MOST PROBLEMS SOLVE THEMSELVES

Owner Mentors Press,
a div. of Brad Poulos Holdings Inc.
Send feedback to publisher@ownermentors.com

ISBN: 978-1-0690996-5-5 (hardcover)

ISBN: 978-1-0690996-3-1 (e-book)

ISBN: 978-1-0690996-4-8 (paperback)

Cover design by Ali Imran

**Owner
Mentors
Press**

The information herein contained is intended as a general reference tool for understanding the underlying principles and practices of the subject matter covered. The opinions and ideas expressed herein are solely those of the author. The author and publisher are not engaged in rendering legal, financial, accounting, tax, insurance, investment or other professional advice or services in this publication. This publication is not intended to provide a basis for action in particular circumstances without consideration by a competent professional. The strategies outlined in this book may not be suitable for every individual or organization and are not guaranteed or warranted to produce any particular results. Further, any examples or sample forms presented are intended merely as illustrations.

The author, publisher and their agents assume no responsibility for errors or omissions and expressly disclaim any responsibility for any liability, loss or risk, personal or otherwise, which is incurred as a consequence, directly or indirectly, of the use and application of any of the contents of this book.

All inquiries should be addressed to :
Owner Mentors Press, a div. of Brad Poulos Holdings Inc.
20 Clovercrest Drive, Brampton, Ontario, Canada. L7A 2N2

Interested in bulk purchases of *Most Problems Solve Themselves*? Contact the publisher for available discount details.

MOST PROBLEMS SOLVE THEMSELVES

*And 51 other **Ideas Worth Stealing** from the Small Business Professor*

Brad Poulos, M.B.A.

Owner Mentors Press

Brampton, Ontario, Canada

To my students, who constantly challenge me to stay sharp, honest, and relevant.

And to my clients, the small business operators, my heroes, who fearlessly drive their businesses forward, often against the odds.

Foreword

The last thing any entrepreneur needs is another book by a celebrity founder or renowned business executive telling stories of their brilliance (they're never just "lucky"), and exhorting readers to work harder and smarter (whatever that means) to become more like them. What is much more difficult to find (and is far more valuable) is guidance that comes from someone who has actually launched and grown many businesses through difficult times, managed the crises, made payroll, juggled suppliers, wrestled with regulators, and lived with the consequences of their decisions. This book is that rarer and more valuable thing: a collection of insights earned the hard way, grounded in research evidence, sharpened by experience, and offered with generosity that is typical of its author.

I've known Brad for thirty years. We met in MBA school, where it was immediately apparent that he had the kind of judgment and practical intelligence that can't really be taught. While the rest of us were still sorting out discounted cash flows and debating case studies, Brad already understood how businesses worked because he had already spent years actually running them. His questions in class were the sort that made professors pause and double-check their notes. His comments were equal parts sharp analysis and wry humour, delivered with a tone that made you realize he'd already tried what the textbooks suggested and had some better ideas.

Over the decades since, Brad has launched, grown, fixed, sold, and advised more businesses than most professors ever encounter. He has succeeded impressively, failed honestly, learned deeply, and – most importantly – reflected on those experiences with uncommon clarity. And he has always been willing to share that knowledge, not in a grand or self-important way, but with the calm confidence of someone who knows that practical wisdom only matters when it's put to use.

This generosity is something I've witnessed repeatedly. I've seen Brad offer sound, actionable advice to young entrepreneurs who approached him nervously after class. I've seen him mentor a new founder through a crisis, not with platitudes but with concrete steps and a real sense of perspective. His default orientation is problem-solving and kindness. He doesn't hoard his hard-won insights; he hands them out freely, with good humour and without ego.

That spirit permeates this entire book.

This book is not a theoretical treatise, though it aligns remarkably well with what the academic research tells us about how small businesses succeed. And it is not simply a collection of war stories presented as universal truths. Instead, it is a rare blend of experience and evidence – practical advice grounded in real operations, shaped by academic knowledge, and filtered through the seasoned judgment of someone who knows firsthand what works, what doesn't, and why.

As someone who has made a career studying entrepreneurs, I find this especially refreshing. Academics are trained to discover patterns across many firms, but entrepreneurs learn from the intense feedback of their own individual experience. Brad bridges these worlds with unusual ease. He knows the research literature, but he also knows the lived reality behind it – the messiness of imperfect information, the improvisation of ad hoc solutions, and the urgency of making tough decisions that can make or break a business. Here he delivers this knowledge with clarity and humour, avoiding both the dryness of pure theory and the bravado and self-justification that too often accompanies books written by executives.

Our friendship and collaboration over the past three decades have only deepened my respect for the way Brad approaches problem-solving. We come from complementary angles: I bring more of the academic analytical scaffolding, and he brings the operational instincts that only years of practice can build. Working together has shown me how well these perspectives fit. As you read this book, you'll see the same combination at work: practical steps, thoughtful reflections, and an underlying commitment to helping entrepreneurs succeed on their own terms.

This book is not a simple recipe or a gimmicky framework. Instead, you'll find something better: a set of insights, attitudes, and habits to help you navigate the unpredictable world of small business with greater confidence and clarity. Brad writes the way he talks: plainly, engagingly, and with a tone that shows you that you're reading someone who has been there and who knows what he's talking about. But the advice here is meant to be used, not just admired from a distance. It is immediately actionable, grounded in the realities of running a business, and delivered with an honesty that entrepreneurs will appreciate.

So, whether you are just thinking of launching your first venture or you've been at this for years, I think you'll find this book to be hugely valuable: practical wisdom drawn from experience, explained with humour, and presented with the intention of helping you to avoid common pitfalls and to build a better business.

You're in good hands. Brad is one of the most insightful and genuine business minds I've ever known. I respect his judgment and admire his clarity, and I'm delighted to see his hard-won knowledge gathered here in one place. I hope you find it as helpful, as encouraging, and as refreshingly down-to-earth as I do.

Dave Valliere, PhD
Professor of Entrepreneurship & Strategy
Toronto, Canada
December 2025

Contents

Introduction

Opening Thoughts

Why Another Business Book?

Because We All Can Use a Better Toolbox.

Years ago, I was running a business with about 50 employees and strong revenue growth, and spent more than one Thursday night tossing and turning about making payroll on Friday morning. We pulled so many rabbits out of a hat in those days!

The worst part? We weren't failing. We had customers. We were profitable on paper. But paper doesn't make payroll.

Despite having an M.B.A. and reading my share of popular business books, I never really understood what that feels like until it was my own ass on the line. Hopefully reading this and the many other stories in this book will help you skip some of the hard, unsexy lessons that they convey.

Around the same time that I was sweating over payroll a friend of mine, let's call him Steve, was exiting his startup He'd built a Toronto-based software company that was being acquired by a much larger firm in Boston. It was the dream scenario: years of grinding finally paying off.

There were five shareholders. One of them, the sales manager, owned just 5%. He wasn't critical to operations, but his signature was required to close, because the buyer wanted 100% ownership.

The night before closing, that sales manager cornered Steve and demanded fifty grand for his signature. Not because the deal was unfair. Not because of some noble principle. But merely because he could.

Steve didn't have a shareholders' agreement and had no time to lawyer up.

Just one opportunist holding the entire deal hostage. So they paid him.

And that's why you always have a shareholders' agreement.

Who This Book Is For

It's for people who have been through situations like the two I just outlined.

If you own or manage a small to medium-sized business, say 25 to 100 employees, or $2 to $30 million in revenue, this book is for you. You're not a startup founder chasing unicorn status, and you're not a Fortune 500 exec with a strategy department and an army of MBAs.

You're running a real business. And some days it feels like it's trying to kill you.

This book is also useful for the people around you, managers, advisors, students of business, but make no mistake: the focus here is on the owner or operator of a small to medium-sized business.

What This Book Is

This is a curated collection of blog posts I've written over the years, grouped by theme and lightly updated. The title is based on the key message in one of them. Many of these articles contain ideas that I have stolen from someone smarter than I am.[1]

Some chapters are drawn from my own screw-ups. Some are things I've learned from peers, students, clients, and in boardrooms. Some contain theoretical concepts that I think are helpful to the audience.

What makes this book a bit different is that it's personal. This is not a neutral, well-balanced resource. It's full of opinions. Mine. Sometimes strong ones.

I'm not claiming universal truth. I offer only what I've learned, what I've seen, and what I think matters. Use what helps.

Why This Book? Why Now? Why Me?

Across my career—running companies, sitting on boards, and teaching thousands of entrepreneurship students—I kept seeing the same problems. Not technical ones. Operator ones.

Cash flow that mysteriously vanishes. Shareholders turning into hostages. Growth that buries a business instead of building it.

So I started writing. First for myself. Then for others. And eventually, I realized I had enough content—and enough people asking for more—that a book made sense.

---

1 *Where possible I try to attribute. For safety's sake, assume I stole all of it!*

Also: I like writing. I like teaching. And yes, I probably like the sound of my own voice just a little too much.

The book contains 52 short chapters, each designed to stand alone. They're grouped into themes like Finance, Management, Ownership, and a few others that emerged naturally from the chaos.

You can read them in order, pick a section that's relevant to you today, or treat it like a weekly gut-check. Feel free to just bounce around based on the article titles that interest you.

No rules. No fluff. Just one operator's take on how to run a business without losing your mind (or your shirt).

I hope you'll highlight, disagree, write swear words in the margins. Feel free to engage with me on social media (LinkedIn) or via the website!

You know your business. You've made it this far for a reason. My hope is simply that a few of these ideas sharpen your edge, spark a useful shift in perspective, or give you a better way to handle something you already deal with daily.

Let's get started.

ENTREPRENEURSHIP

10 things to consider before becoming an entrepreneur

Originally posted on April 5, 2011.

The following top 10 list is adapted from Carol Roth's book *The Entrepreneur Equation*.

Are you tired of working for someone else? Do you think starting your own business could set you free?

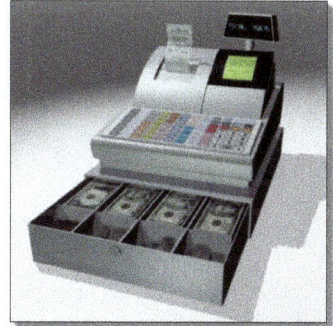

Think again! The failure rate for new businesses is gloomy.

In fact, the great majority of businesses (up to 90%) fail within five years.

The reality is that the average business does less than $100,000 in sales, is not innovative, and has no plans for growth (from Professor Scott Shane, in his book *The Illusions of Entrepreneurship*). The majority of businesses (60%) do not earn a profit over their lifetime.

> *Yet despite incredibly high failure rates, over 6 million people start a business each year. Before you decide to join the ranks of the self-employed, find out if business ownership is right for you.*

Are you ready to be an entrepreneur? Consider these 10 steps.

1. Define your motivation.

Ask yourself why you really want to start a business. Are you looking to get rich quick? Do you want to showcase your talent or service? Are you tired of your boss taking credit for what you do? These are not reasons to start a business. On the other hand, if you love the idea of running an entity, if you like creating systems and procedures, adore servicing customers, and if you thrive on wearing many different hats and balancing responsibilities, then entrepreneurship may be something to look into.

2. Say hello to your new boss.

Wait, I thought I was in charge now. Not exactly. When you start your own business, you are no longer in control. And, you may not have the freedom you think you do. See, you are controlled by your customers, investors, and lenders – and you are personally responsible for answering to all of them, all of the time.

3.   Evaluate how well you work with others.

Many people dream of opening a business as an escape – from the annoying coworker who won't leave you alone, or from an overbearing boss. But having a business doesn't mean you no longer have to interface with people. In fact, it's the opposite. To get clients, investors, and others to help you with your business (including accountants, lawyers, and more) you'll need to keep your people skills sharp.

4.   Add up your responsibilities.

Owning a business is very much like raising a child. It's a 24/7 job. Will you be able to respond immediately when your "child" has an emergency? If anything happens to the business (including a loss of your investment money and income), how will it affect your family or home life? Consider the worst-case scenarios when evaluating your responsibilities and impact to your current lifestyle.

5.   Look at your management and industry experience.

Being able to manage employees and vendors is the type of entrepreneurial skill you'll need to acquire before starting your own business. You'll also need to know your industry inside and out, including aspects you may not be familiar with or may not even like, including marketing, accounting, and more. Don't have the experience you need? Spend time working in a similar company, shadow a business owner in your industry, or accept an internship. Test the waters first with a trial run before you start your own company.

6. Take stock of whom you know.

Business comes down to not what you know, but whom you know. If you don't know many people, you may be tempted to overlook just how important it is to network and be connected. But good connections are worth their weight in gold. They will get you interest from investors and lenders. You'll receive better financing, prices, terms, and conditions from business suppliers and professional services. And you'll receive more customer referrals. This is driven home in *Effectual Entrepreneurship*, the iconic book by Professor Saras Sarasvathy of the University of Virginia's Darden School.

7. Be honest about your relationship with money.

Are you financially responsible? Do you have any money to invest in your business, or will you be relying on others? Do you panic about spending money or avoid financial risk at all costs? Don't expect your relationship with money to change just because you've opened a business. Opening a business requires money — enough for you to start, operate the business and to live on — as well as sound financial management.

8. Assess your personality type.

Do you prefer the "status quo" and like to avoid the unexpected? Can you handle a life of highs and lows – including financial highs and lows? Could your savings and bank account handle financial lows as well? If you are a person who likes stability and control, or if you prefer when things go as planned, the roller-coaster ride of a new business may not be right for you.

9. Examine the marketplace and your competition.

Before you leap into entrepreneurship, take a hard look at the marketplace and your competition. Is your market saturated with successful businesses? Is your industry littered with so many bad businesses that it's developed a bad reputation? Both good and bad competitors will influence just how successful your business will be. You will need to market and brand your business to shine above the good competitors, and to make up for the bad ones.

10. Test your scalability.

The most successful businesses rely on automation and delegation. Will other employees be able to do your work? If not, can you teach others what to do in an easy-to-follow format? If your business relies on your skills – and your skills alone – you might have a successful job, but not a successful business.

Original post URL: https://bradpoulos.com/10-things-to-consider-before-becoming-an-entrepreneur/

10 Tips for New Entrepreneurs – Sure Ways to Increase Your Chances of Success

Originally posted on June 20, 2011.

Are you a new entrepreneur or thinking of taking the plunge?
Here are 10 sure-fire ways to increase the chances that your new venture is successful.

"Look what I found in the dumpster! A perfectly good business plan!"

1. Make sure you are ready, and other key stakeholders in your life are too!

Owning and running your own business is neither easy nor boring. It surely is not for everyone. Each person's situation is unique, but most of us need some kind of safety net, whether that be at home to handle overload duties with the family, or financially. Ensure that your income is either not vital to your monthly living, or is going to be covered through savings to the extent that your business doesn't replace your pre-entrepreneurial income.
You must also make sure you are ready for the time investment which can be immense at times, and for the sacrifices that will surely have to be made. You may not be able to play on that pickup hockey team or sandlot baseball team on Saturday mornings any more – but you should try to maintain some balance as much as you can. Finally, ensure that you have the necessary skills, or have ready access to them through your network.

2. Have a clear vision and make sure it's understood

Without a clear, written, well-articulated goal or goals for yourself and your business, how do you know what do when you get up each morning? Too many people today sit around waiting for their email to tell them to do something! Applying the military analogy of "Commander's Intent", it is much more effective to empower your team and your company and yourself with three things – purpose, resources, desired end state – and let them deal with the myriad possibly interim difficulties and required changes to their own plans.

3. Have a business plan, and monitor/update it regularly

Getting into this kind of routine early in your entrepreneurial venture is important discipline for several reasons. It prepares you for the day when outside investors will demand it. It also helps you quickly test your assumptions regarding what kind of revenue and expenses you will have in your business. Regularly updating a business plan is vital if you are going to seriously use it. At least annually.

4. Work your network hard both before and after starting your business

People want to help. Studies have shown that at least 80% of the time people will help you, if you *ask*! Your personal network is one of your most valuable assets. Use it! One of the biggest mistakes I have made myself, and I have seen made over the years, is not asking for all the help you need. So figure out how your friends and acquaintances can assist your venture and ask for that referral, piece of information or introduction. And don't forget to work into every networking opportunity an offer to help the other person in some way.

5. Never forget "If it doesn't jingle, it doesn't count!"

.I first heard that from my finance professor, Jim Hatch. It basically means cash is more important than virtually everything else. Without cash your business sputters and eventually dies. All the sales in the world won't help you if they are sitting in a poor quality receivable. And just *try* to buy a new car with EBITDA or Net Income!

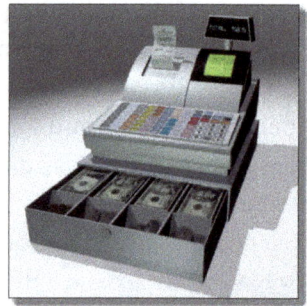

6. No business is too small to do things right

I was once very impressed to see a restauranteur with one location who had an operations manual that would have impressed Ray Kroc. This was about 17 years ago and for the record that restaurant is still thriving. This man had read Michael Gerber's The E-Myth and understood that by working "on" his business a little, he could make it so that almost anyone with the right attitude could work "in" it. No one person was or is vital to the operation on a daily basis, including the entrepreneur, once you get this formula right.

7. Put off hiring employees as long as you can, and then hire the best you can find

It takes some courage to consistently hire people who you feel are "better" than you are, but that's what successful entrepreneurs do. Once you have decided you must take the plunge and hire that first (or next) employee, then be sure you know what you need and want in that position, and be ruthless about not settling for less. A wrong hiring decision is almost never the band-aid you want it to be, and can be expensive and time-draining to make right, not to mention the unfairness to the person that you put in the wrong position. Find the budget to get the person you need and then let them shine. You will make mistakes. When you do fix them swiftly and fairly.

8. Don't involve the bank unless you absolutely have to

The bank is almost never really your friend. Wall Street Merchant bankers' greed in the decade or two prior to 2008 created such a huge implosion of available capital, especially to small business, that there is still no end in sight in terms of real commercial lending to small business. What happens in reality is the bank loans the money to the owner, but takes no real risk in terms of the business. Not until your business is much larger and the threat of moving your business is enough to get personal guarantees removed. If you can, bootstrap your venture and don't load it with debt unless you must.

9. Be prepared to admit mistakes and do it quickly

Thomas Watson, founder of IBM said something along the lines of:

Would you like me to give you a formula for... success? It's quite simple, really. Double your rate of failure. You're thinking of failure as the enemy of success. But it isn't at all... you can be discouraged by failure / or you can learn from it. So go ahead and make mistakes. Make all you can. Because, remember that's where you'll find success. On the far side.

You can't be afraid to make mistakes, and you have to be able to quickly recognize them and deal with them. Not every idea you try will be successful. But as Mr. Watson said, it's on the other side of those failures that you will find the right formula.

10. Have Fun!

If you are not having fun doing what you are doing, what really is the point? If money and bragging rights are more important to you than getting satisfaction out of what you do and how you do it, then the grind of the entrepreneurial world may not be the right place for you. Perhaps a corporate job would be better. I have always found that the environments where there is a commitment to results coupled with a positive atmosphere are the high performance places to work.

Original post URL: https://bradpoulos.com/10-tips-for-new-entrepreneurs/

Your Biggest Competitor Isn't Who You Think

Originally posted on September 9, 2025

Hidden Competition Leads to Creative Destruction

In 2000, Kodak still dominated the photography business. They saw Fuji as the big rival, and their boardrooms obsessed over film quality and price. But Kodak didn't die because of Fuji. The killer came from outside: digital cameras, that eventually had their own lunches eaten by smartphones. A similar story can be told of independent video stores. Their owners were losing sleep over the prospect of the big bad Blockbuster coming to the neighbourhood, while Netflix first changed the game with mail order rentals, and then together with other streaming services put them right out of business.

That's the danger of creative destruction. The real threats don't come from the shop across the street. They come from outsiders who rewrite the rules while you're busy watching your obvious rivals. And owing to the technological advances of the past several generations, we have seen many examples in our everyday lives.

The post office lost volume to the fax machine which was made mostly redundant by email. Alongside that was the typewriter that was first supplanted by the dedicated word processor whose demise was sealed by the PC.

The Nature of Creative Destruction

In his 1942 book *Capitalism, Socialism and Democracy*, economist Joseph Schumpeter coined the phrase "creative destruction" to describe how innovation constantly reshapes markets. New businesses, technologies, and ideas rise up to replace the old. Not in any malicious sense but rather in the natural cycle of progress, like a forest fire is part of a natural growth, destruction, and renewal process.

The problem is that you can't fight what you don't see. Most businesses spend their time looking horizontally, at competitors who look like them. Restaurants obsess over other restaurants. Bookstores watch other bookstores. But disruption usually comes diagonally, from someone solving the same customer problem in a completely different way. The blind spot is costly. Billions get spent defending against the wrong enemy.

Why We Miss the Hidden Competitors

First and foremost, it's easy and comforting to focus on beating existing competitors. It feels familiar, so we keep fighting the same battle, and don't necessarily watch our flank as we should.

There's a psychological trap: it's tempting to dismiss outsiders as "not real competitors." Taxi companies said Uber was illegal, and attempted to dismiss them, hoping they'd go away. Uber responded by becoming legal, and put a massive dent in the taxi industry by offering a package of services that people valued more.

How to See What's Coming

The other reason we miss hidden competitors is because they are hidden. Until they're not. It's a rare person who can spot these often cataclysmic industry changes before they happen. But some business owners keep missing these threats as they happen. The smart operator will have a broad worldview and a wide variety of inputs of new information so that they spot trends early (or hear from those who have). A few pointers:

- Consume a steady diet of mainstream news, trade or industry information, podcasts, business and political news, and even a bit of popular culture. Be among the first in your game to know what's coming, and be aware of your own biases so you avoid dismissing threats. The current buzz around AI will surely lead to major disruptions in some industries, and small businesses operating in those domains are better positioned to adjust than larger ones. Do it early.

- Keep your eyes open to customer behaviour, not industry boundaries. Customers don't want a taxi; they want mobility. They don't want a hotel; they want a bed and a safe place to stay. And they don't want a travel agent; they want to book a vacation. When you frame it that way, more substitutes become visible.

- Watch the fringes. Early adopters and subcultures often preview the next wave. Teenagers embraced TikTok before adults realized it was more than lip-sync videos. By the time businesses woke up and created YouTube Shorts and Instagram Reels, TikTok had reshaped how an entire generation consumes media.

- Study nontraditional rivals. Ask: "If my customers didn't use me, what would they do instead?" The answers are rarely the competitor you obsess over. A restaurant might lose a customer not to another restaurant, but to a meal kit subscription or a grocery store with hot meals.

- Practice institutional humility. Assume the next threat is invisible right now. If your business strategy is built entirely around fighting today's known competitors, you're leaving yourself exposed.

Don't Get Blindsided

It'll rarely be the direct competitor that kills you. The danger is from the outsider who rewrites the rules while you're focused on the familiar battle. Small or large, every business owner needs to widen their radar. Pay attention to shifts in customer behavior, new technologies, and alternative ways people meet the need you serve.

You likely can't prevent the creative destruction of your industry, but you can foresee it, if you're looking.

Original post URL: https://bradpoulos.com/creative-destruction/

Bootstrapping: Building Your Business on Your Terms

Originally posted on September 27 2025.

The Bootstrap Reality Check

In the startup world, bootstrapping is more than a tactic. It's a rite of passage. Building from scratch with little more than savings, sweat, and sheer determination is practically a badge of honour. It demands courage, tenacity, and a willingness to survive on fumes while proving your idea has legs. Bootstrapping forces you to treat every dollar as sacred, validate every decision with customers, and earn your right to grow. But cling too tightly, and what once fueled your launch can quietly become the anchor that holds you back.

Most bootstrap journeys start small: personal savings, maybe a day job to pay the bills, and profits funnelled straight back into the business. Pre-sales, crowdfunding, or bartering help bridge gaps when cash is scarce. The upside is clear—complete ownership, customer-driven decision making, and ironclad financial discipline. The downsides are just as real: growth is gradual, cash flow tight, risk personal, and hiring talent harder without big-company perks. Bootstrapping builds resilience, but it also leaves scars.

The goal isn't to deprive your business of resources. It's about maximizing the productivity of every dollar until your money generates more value than your labour alone.

The Psychology Behind the Bootstrap

Bootstrapping transcends mere cost-cutting; it's about strategic precision. This approach demands unwavering discipline to resist distractions, creative problem-solving to navigate obstacles with limited resources, and the mental fortitude to operate under constant uncertainty. In those formative years, founders guard their control and equity fiercely, driven by the intoxicating combination of ownership, autonomy, and the satisfaction of declaring: "I built this on my own terms." Yet some entrepreneurs push this philosophy too far, creating what might be called the perpetual bootstrap trap. This mindset permeates organizational culture, creating environments that prize pragmatism over polish and substance over spectacle. Bootstrap companies invest in impact, not appearances. Profitability takes precedence over publicity.

Jeff Bezos's legendary door-desk wasn't just furniture; it was a cultural statement. At Amazon, frugality and resourcefulness weren't temporary hacks. They were principles that shaped how the company operated. You don't need Amazon's scale to see the lesson.

Whether you're running a kitchen-table startup or a $10M company, resourcefulness is cultural, not just financial.

Amazon's eventual "every day is Day 1" philosophy emerged from this foundation, insisting that innovation, agility, and scrappiness must persist even when bootstrapping becomes unnecessary. Clinging to bootstrap methods a decade into your journey isn't admirable. It's alarming. It signals either market limitations, stagnant growth, or paralysis in the face of scaling opportunities. Bootstrapping that drags on forever becomes a cage.

Lessons From Legends

Each started scrappy. And each eventually moved beyond pure bootstrapping. That's the key. Bootstrapping is the launch strategy, not the mission. But the one thing they all did was create intimate relationships with their customers, truly co-creating with them.

Mailchimp initially offered a free version of their email marketing service, attracting a large user base with a limited marketing budget, then relied heavily on customer feedback to improve their product.

SparkFun Electronics started in a dorm room when the founder, Nathan Seidle, couldn't find the electronic components he needed for his own projects. He began by solving his own problem (or what I call "scratching his own itch"), sold directly through their website, kept margins higher by bypassing traditional distribution channels, and invested heavily in tutorials, guides, and educational materials, which helped build community and drive organic traffic. They reinvested profits back into inventory and operations rather than seeking external funding.

Tough Mudder created a unique and challenging obstacle course race that stood out from other fitness events. They relied heavily on word of mouth and social media to spread the word about their events, leveraging the excitement and stories of participants to attract new customers.

What these companies had in common wasn't thrift alone. They listened obsessively to customers, built communities around their products, and reinvested every dollar back into making the experience better. That's the essence of bootstrapping done right.

The Legacy

Bootstrapping is empowering, but it's not a life sentence. It's the fuel for takeoff, not the entire flight plan. The question isn't whether you can raise money—it's whether you've built something worth funding in the first place. Bootstrapping forces you to answer that question honestly. Once you've proven it, don't be afraid to graduate.

Build lean, build strong, and then scale on your own terms.

Original post URL: https://bradpoulos.com/bootstrapping/

We Always Overshoot: From Fiber to Cannabis to AI

Originally posted on October 4, 2025.

Every generation believes it has discovered the "next big thing." Railroads in the 1870s, fiber optics and the dotcom's irrational exuberance in the 1990s, cannabis in the 2010s, and today's artificial intelligence boom all shared the same pattern: investors raced ahead of real demand. The technology was never fake. The timing was.

I watched two of these booms from inside the industry: the dot-com fiber glut and the Canadian cannabis overbuild. In both cases, exuberance pushed supply far beyond what the market could handle, destroying capital but laying foundations for future growth. I spotted the cannabis overshoot a year before the crash because I lived through the fibre glut. I see the same signals now in AI.

A Familiar Pattern

In the late 1990s, the "information superhighway" was the rallying cry. Companies raced to trench streets and string fiber, convinced the internet would consume bandwidth faster than anyone could build it. I remember telling my staff that the telcos were throwing money out the window of their ivory towers and our job was to run around and catch as much as we could.

The scale was breathtaking. We knew internet traffic was growing fast, but we also knew the physics of laying fiber: once you've dug the trench, adding more strands costs very little. The result was a massive overshoot of capacity.

By 2002, after the bubble burst, only about 3% of U.S. fiber capacity was actually lit. By 2005, it was still under 5%, and most of those gleaming strands sat "dark" for years. Lighting them required investment in costly electronics, and demand wasn't anywhere near the levels promised in the pitch decks of 1999. By 2012 only half of that laid fibre was being used to carry traffic.

The consequences for telecom carriers were brutal. Giants like Global Crossing and WorldCom went bankrupt. Investors lost billions.

Those once-dark fibers became the backbone of the modern internet. It took over a decade, but the glut eventually turned into the infrastructure we rely on today.

The Cannabis Overbuild in Canada

Fast-forward to 2017. Canada was on the brink of legalizing recreational cannabis, and the capital markets responded with a wave of exuberance. Billions of dollars poured into greenhouses, indoor cultivation facilities, and grandiose promises of global domination.

I was close to that market too, and the mismatch was obvious. Demand was real, but projections were wildly inflated. Consumer adoption was steady, not exponential, and regulations slowed distribution. Yet companies raced to build capacity as if every Canadian were going to double their consumption overnight.

That summer, I was warning publicly that there was far more production capacity than the market could absorb. Within a year, the crash arrived. Wholesale cannabis prices collapsed. Many facilities were mothballed before they ever planted a single crop. Companies wrote off billions, and stock prices cratered.

The lesson was the same as with fiber: the product was real, the enthusiasm understandable, but the buildout raced far ahead of demand.

Déjà Vu: The AI Buildout

Today, I feel that same twinge of recognition. The AI boom has unleashed a global arms race.

Trillions in projected spending are being funneled into GPUs, datacenters, and energy infrastructure. The numbers are staggering

UBS estimates companies will spend US$375B globally on AI infrastructure in 2025 alone (NYT). Further, Nvidia CEO Jensen Huang now sees $3–4 trillion cumulative AI infrastructure spend by the end of this decade.

Contrast that with revenue estimates of $20-25 billion for this year and, being optimistic, $60 billion by next year; far off what's needed to justify the invested trillions!   (Sources: Bloomberg, Statista, and McKinsey)

Why We Always Overshoot

This cycle is not an accident. Cheap capital, fear of missing out, and the "land grab" logic of emerging technologies combine to drive investment ahead of real adoption. Psychologically, we humans overestimate what will happen in the short term and underestimate what will happen in the long term.

We're in an AI Bubble

Just last month no less than Sam Altman, CEO of AI industry giant OpenAI, unequivocally stated that we're in a bubble. To be fair, he further stated that all of the bubbles of the past were indeed about things that were a big deal. It's just that people get overexcited. There's no doubt that AI is a big deal.

The chart below shows the iSTOXX AI Global Artificial Intelligence Large 100 Index (an index of 100 companies that invest in AI). The fact that we're at an all-time high doesn't alone warrant such pessimism. It's the disconnect between revenues and the investment being made to earn them.

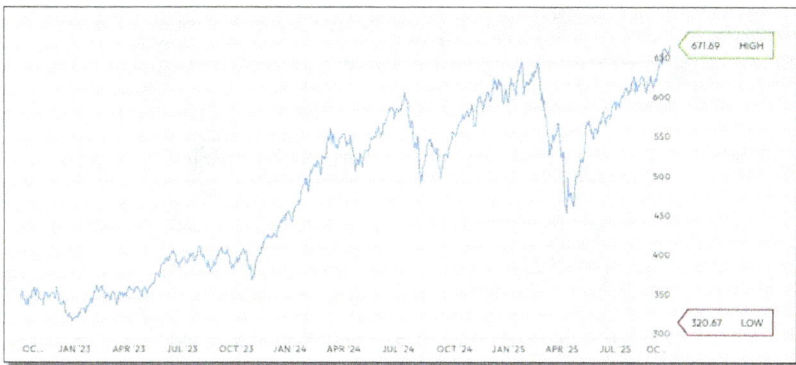

Source: https://stoxx.com/index/ixagal1p/

We will see some of the same consequences we saw with fiber and cannabis: bankruptcies, stranded assets, and disappointed investors. The market will punish the weakest players and the most overextended bets. But AI does have one crucial difference. Fiber strands buried in the ground couldn't easily be moved, and cannabis grow ops couldn't be repurposed for much else. Computing capacity, by contrast, is fungible. A datacentre built for AI can pivot to scientific computing, enterprise IT, climate modelling, or healthcare workloads. GPUs that aren't training large language models can still crunch numbers for countless other industries. That doesn't mean investors will escape losses. Even if the capital is redeployed and the economic waste is less severe and permanent, the AI bubble will burst, and the revenues will never justify the investment being made at present. There's no doubt that the capacity being built today will eventually be redeployed, just as fiber was lit, years later. The question is how much capital will be destroyed before that happens.

One More Parallel

The mismatch between capital invested and realistic revenues isn't the only common thread with earlier bubbles. The crash of 1929, the dot-com mania, and Canada's cannabis green rush all saw a surge of retail investors piling in. I remember lots of small players buying on margin and day-trading chasing internet stocks, and in my world everyone was buying weed stocks in the mid 20-teens. All of these were just before the market collapsed.

What If I'm Wrong

This is one that's akin to Pascal's Wager. If I'm wrong, there's no downside. I'm not shorting these stocks or recommending that you do! If I'm right, forewarned is forearmed..

Original post URL: https://bradpoulos.com/ai-overbuild/

Choosing the Right Business Owner Title

Originally posted on October 14, 2025.

Why You're Probably Not a CEO (And That's Okay)

A potential client will form a (reliable) first impression less than one second after meeting you. Your business title is often the first thing they notice, shaping how they perceive both you and your company. Overstating your title will immediately undermine your reputation.

> *"So, I see you're a CEO. Is your title overstated, or do you just work for a really small company?"*

Title clarity beats vanity every time

Who Cares? Pretty much everyone. Your title influences how clients, partners, and employees perceive your authority and expertise. It's a reflection of your company culture and working environment, but it also says something about YOU. It's rare that we can choose our own title in the corporate world, however as the owner of the company, you have full reign over what to call yourself. Your choice will reveal something about how you view yourself.

The right title communicates your role, establishes credibility, and signals what people can expect when working with you. Choose wisely, because your title creates immediate associations: "CEO" suggests a larger corporation, while "Founder" implies hands-on involvement and entrepreneurial spirit. Managing Director is quite formal and conveys gravity.

Your title should reflect your business structure. An LLC owner's title differs from a corporation's CEO. It also gives some idea of your daily role. As such, it can evolve as the company does. Scale your title along with the company.

So, Which Title, When?

Let's start with the elephant in the room. I have met many solopreneurs who use the CEO title. This is categorically wrong. CEO stands for Chief

Executive Officer. Chief implies you're leading other executives. No CFO? No CTO? Then you're not the CEO.

I have used the titles of President, Founder & Vice-President, and Director in companies that I started or helped start. The only time I have used the CEO title is when I was running a public company, and had a COO, CFO and a CTO reporting to me.

The exception would be a startup where the intention from the outset is to go big and create a team to raise serious money.

Middle Ground

If not CEO, then what? Most small business operators should probably use one of the following titles: President, General Manager, Managing Director, or Owner. I'm not a fan of the latter because it's not an operational description. It says nothing about the role the person plays. The others are somewhat interchangeable.

You should let the industry drive this to some degree as well. Some industries are more formal than others, and demand a more formal-sounding title, or just cry out for a different title (creative industries for example).

Less Is More

Titles don't have to be flashy—or even accurate in a legal sense. I've known many business owners that deliberately understate their titles, and don't broadcast that they have a second function—owner—in addition to their operational role. Examples I have seen include Business Development Manager, Director of Sales, Creative Director, and, when the owner was the technical lead, Technical Director.

Other titles, like Founder for example, might fit when the person has less of a day-to-day role, and the company wants to honour their early role as a vital player.

If you're in a consulting company or other kind of professional service firm, the term Principal might be a good fit, and if you're the sole owner-operator of a business, handling everything from strategy to daily operations, you might be a Proprietor.

Title	What it Signals
CEO	"This is a larger company with multiple execs"
Founder	"I started this"
President	"I'm the head decision-maker"
Managing Director	"I run the day-to-day and keep the trains running"
General Manager	"I'm responsible for operations and staff"
Owner	"I own this, but who knows what I do day-to-day"
Business Dev Manager	"I'm focused on growth and relationships"
Principal	"I'm the senior professional here"
Technical Director	"I'm the product/tech brains of this operation"

How to Choose

Here are a few "watchouts" for choosing a title:

1. Prioritize clarity – People should immediately understand your role and how to work with you.

2. Match your actual role – Your title should reflect what you actually do daily.

3. Consider perception – Think about what associations your title creates (professional scale, company culture, expertise level).

4. Research industry standards – Align with norms in your sector.

Your title isn't just what's on your business card. It's a test of self-awareness. Nail it, and you signal credibility. Flub it, and you're just another punchline on LinkedIn..

Original post URL: https://bradpoulos.com/business-owner-title/

Then vs. Now: How Entrepreneurship Has Changed—Almost Entirely for the Better

Originally posted on November 11, 2025.

In 1995, I pitched our board of directors for $2 million to launch a business called DirecPC. I had done a bit of business plan work, sketched out our startup costs, and sized the working capital we'd need. I guess for the time, it was a solid enough pitch.

We needed $1 million in capital and $1 million for working capital and marketing. That was it. I had a revenue forecast but had talked to exactly zero potential customers. They knew that, and they were okay with it. In fact, they approved the investment on the spot.

This was Bell Canada's board. Smart people. But this was a different era of entrepreneurship. We hadn't gone lean yet. Most startups back then were built like that: plan-first, customer-later.

Things have changed—and almost entirely for the better.

Why That Would Never Fly Today

Back then:

- Capital was scarce and slow-moving.
- Market research was expensive.
- Business plans and boardroom pitches were the norm.
- We would practice what seemed like responsible planning and do as we were taught in biz school: Ready. Aim. Fire.

The default strategy was:

Idea $\Rightarrow$ raise money $\Rightarrow$ build the thing $\Rightarrow$ launch."

Today, it's the opposite. Now its Ready. Fire. Aim!

Entrepreneurs are expected to validate before building, to start small, to talk to customers early, and to build iteratively. It's not just cheaper. It's smarter. In fact, once I started learning about lean startup 15-20 years ago, I felt kinda dumb for not coming up with the concept myself, and for being responsible for so much "bad" entrepreneurship.

Best Practices In Entrepeneurship in 2025

Here are four ideas that have contributed to the way the game has changed.

1. Effectuation – Start With What You've Got

Instead of starting with a fixed goal and figuring out how to get there, effectual entrepreneurs start with what they have (skills, knowledge, connections), and let outcomes emerge from action.

Ask: "Given who I am, what I know, what I have and who I know, what can I do?"

This mindset, the brainchild of Darden Prof. Saras Sarasvathy, is practical, adaptive, and resource-conscious.

Example: Sara Blakely started Spanx with $5,000 in savings, no fashion industry experience, and one key insight from her own frustration with pantyhose. She didn't try to become a fashion mogul. She used what she had—a sales background, an understanding of women's clothing frustrations, and sheer persistence—to cold-call hosiery mills and pitch buyers at Neiman Marcus herself. The business emerged from what was available to her, not from a grand plan.

This mindset is powerful because it removes the "I need X before I can start" barrier. You don't need venture capital, industry credentials, or perfect conditions. You need to start with what's in front of you.

You can get more a more detailed explanation along with resources and case studies here.

2. Bricolage – Build With What's Lying Around

Think of bricolage as entrepreneurial MacGyver-ing[2]. You improvise using whatever resources are on hand. You don't wait for perfect conditions. You repurpose, recombine, and reframe. It's a close cousin of effectuation.

Perfect is expensive. Bricolage is fast, cheap, and often good enough to get started.

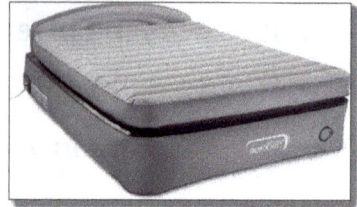

Example: Airbnb's founders couldn't afford rent for their San Francisco apartment. They bought air mattresses, set up a basic website in a weekend, and rented floor space to conference attendees. They didn't wait to build a hospitality empire. they used three air mattresses and a domain name. The "bed and breakfast" part came from offering Pop-Tarts for breakfast. That scrappy MVP eventually became a $100 billion company.

For many modern founders, this is how the first version of the business comes to life. You use free tools, borrow equipment, trade services, test on friends. You make it work with what you've got.

3. Lean Startup – Validate Before You Build

Popularized by Eric Ries, Lean Startup thinking introduced a simple but transformative idea: test before you invest.

The concepts of a Build → Measure → Learn loop, the Minimum Viable Product (MVP) and "customer discovery" all have their roots in the Lean Startup. Now we get real feedback from real users before making large commitments.

Example: Dropbox didn't build their entire cloud storage infrastructure before knowing if anyone wanted it. Drew

---

[2] *MacGyver was a 1980s TV series about a resourceful agent who improvised clever solutions from seemingly trivial items, so popular that his name was verbed.*

Houston created a 3-minute demo video showing how the product would work and posted it to Hacker News. Overnight, their beta waiting list went from 5,000 to 75,000 people. He validated massive demand with a video before writing most of the code.

You don't build something massive and hope it works. Lean forces you to make small bets, learn quickly, and adjust as needed. Each iteration should answer a specific question: Will people pay for this? Do they use this feature? What's the biggest friction point?

Sadly, it's still not widely understood. I have watched those close to me make the mistake of building a solution without a problem three times since I started teaching lean startup.

4. Blue Ocean Strategy – Compete by Not Competing

Instead of fighting over scraps in a crowded market ("red oceans"), create entirely new market space ("blue oceans") by delivering new value in unexpected ways.

Example: Cirque du Soleil faced a declining circus industry–kids preferred video games, animal rights activists protested animal acts, and star performers commanded huge salaries. Instead of competing harder in the traditional circus space, they eliminated

the animals, reduced the tent/spectacle costs, added theatrical storylines and artistic choreography, and targeted corporate clients and adults willing to pay premium ticket prices. They started playing an entirely different game than Ringling Brothers.

The key is making the competition irrelevant by changing what game you're playing. Other examples are Yellow Tail who made wine approachable for non-wine drinkers and Curves who reinvented gyms specifically for women who were intimidated by traditional alternatives.

What Founders Can Learn From This Shift

The good news, rarely will you need $2 million. You need five real customer conversations, a whiteboard, and maybe a weekend.

Entrepreneurship today is faster, cheaper, more experimental—and far more forgiving. The tools are better. The methods are smarter. The costs of failure are lower. And the feedback loops are tighter.

But what hasn't changed is the mindset. Entrepreneurs still need grit, vision, hustle, and resilience. Those aren't outdated—they're timeless.

Final Thought

We were flying blind in 1995, and it worked. But only because there wasn't a better way.

Today, there is.

Use it.

Original post URL: https://bradpoulos.com/modern-entrepreneurship-strategies

LEADERSHIP

The Five Basic Leadership Principles

Originally posted on June 17 2014.

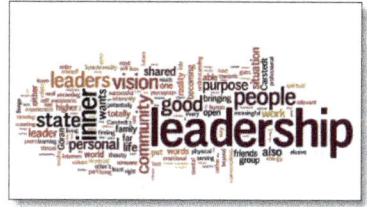

Leadership Principles that Stand the Test of Time

I was very fortunate to be part of an incredible management training program that Telesat put all of its management through back in about 1989 or so, when I was in my first real management job. The key to the program — and the reason it was so effective — was that it was taught by our own senior managers, who had been trained on the material by the company that had created it. My own group was lucky enough to have Barry Turner, one of the brightest men in the company, as our facilitator. Barry later became my boss when he switched over from Space Systems to become VP of Sales and Marketing, but he shone greatest in his role as a Director of Space Systems. Barry was one of the people who encouraged me most to go back to school and get an MBA, and is probably the smartest person I've ever reported to, however, I digress...

The Leadership training program was divided into 16 or 20 modules, each with a theme such as "Dealing with Difficult People" or "Coaching for Effectiveness" or "Setting Goals for Superior Performance". However underlying these modules were the "Five Basic Leadership Principles".

These were the foundation of the entire program, and are quite frankly my main take-aways. They have stuck with me day in and day out for 25 years and I often think about them, partly because they were so important that we were all given coffee mugs with these leadership principles engraved on both sides (thus they applied equally to southpaws as to "normal" folk). I stared at them all day for several years!

Like so many management principles, they are very basic and perhaps particularly empowering because of their simplicity.

Here they are:

1. Focus on the situation, issue, or behavior, not on the person.

2. Maintain the self-confidence and self-esteem of others.

3. Maintain constructive relationships with your employees, peers, and managers.

4. Take initiative to make things better.

5. Lead by example.

These apply equally to life as they do to the business world. I thought they were worth sharing.

Original post URL: https://bradpoulos.com/five-basic-leadership-principles/

You're a F*%&ing Tyrant: My First Lesson in Radical Candor

Originally posted on June 20 2025.

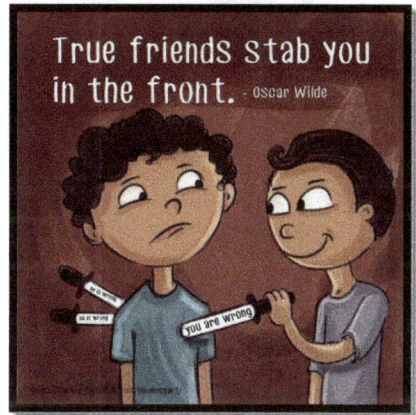

True friends stab you in the front. - Oscar Wilde

I was in my first real management job at age 28, doing performance reviews for the technologists who reported to me. I was in Vancouver, giving my best tech, Geoff, his review. This was the first time I'd done any of this.

Geoff and I were previously peers and friends. We had a huge amount of mutual respect. He had wanted the job that I applied for and got, but I saw little, if any, resentment.

I gave Geoff a glowing review. Why not? He was a star. When we'd finished talking about his review, I very purposefully pushed it to the side, looked at him and said, "OK, now you're done. Please review me."

He said, "Are you sure, Brad?"

"Yeah. Of course. I really respect your opinion."

"Brad. Are you sure?"

"Geoff. Yes. I want to have good two-way communication between us."

"Brad. Are you really sure?"

"Geoff. Yes! Jeez!"

"OK then. You're a fucking tyrant."

That's a word-for-word quote. I will never forget that moment.

It wasn't how I saw myself, but Geoff gave it to me straight. And that moment, long before its creator coined the term, was my first real dose of Radical Candor. It stung. It also shook something loose.

What he gave me was a brutally honest truth bomb, wrapped in respect. That combination made me stop, reflect, and begin to change. It didn't just hit me.

It helped me. So much that I've told this story countless times, and called Geoff a few years ago to thank him, some 35 years after this conversation!

The Radical Candor Framework

Radical Candor is a concept and practice leadership framework created by Kim Scott, and it sits on a deceptively simple two-by-two grid:

- One axis is Care Personally - you give a shit, and that guides how you will approach the current situation.
- The other is Challenge Directly – you're willing to do the uncomfortable but generous thing and tell people what they need to hear.

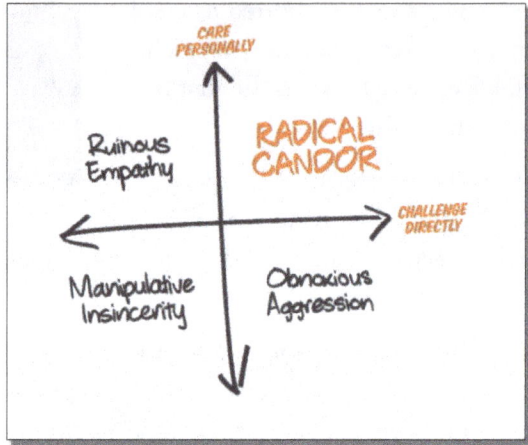

The Radical Candor Framework is a trademark of Radical Candor, LLC.

When you score high on both, you're practicing *Radical Candor.* This is the benchmark. The gold standard. You can maintain a person's dignity while helping them improve or make changes for the better in some way. Not many can!

If you challenge directly but don't show you care, you might be a jerk. This she calls *Obnoxious Aggression.* Interestingly there's some evidence that from a performance point of view, after Radical Candor, this is where your most effective managers will be.

If you care deeply but don't say the hard thing, you're coddling. Or, as Scott calls it, showing *Ruinous Empathy.* Sadly, this is where the majority of managers lie. They care. Just not enough to really help you improve.

Finally, there's the bottom left quadrant, where good intentions are rare, and your problems often germinate. Managers that operate with *Manipulative Insincerity* may prioritize politics, exhibit passive-aggressive behaviour, or simply check out leadership-wise. If you have managers in your organization who live in that quadrant... I have to ask why?

Why Radical Candor Matters for Small Business Owners

In a small business, there's nowhere for subpar performance to hide. The impact of every team member is more palpable than in a large business, so using best-practices in a small business pays off more. Employees respond to genuine feedback intended to develop, and nurture. Fewer will quit. And the ones that stay will outperform your competition. A high-performance culture has to be built on accountability, and keeping it real, among other things. It has to invite open and honest communication while allowing team members to develop personal relationships. When things are moving fast, the clarity and alignment it brings will help keep the team moving in the right direction, together.

Practicing Radical Candor: How to Start

One of the ways I describe this to my students is,

"... it's like Oscar Wilde said... Stabbing someone right in the front!"
-Brad Poulos

Radical Candor isn't just a top-down tool. As a small business owner or leader, you should actively encourage it in the other direction, too. That means inviting your team to challenge you and to tell you when you're off course, when something you did didn't land well, or when your decision-making isn't clear. If you want a culture of truth and trust, it has to work both ways.

1. Build Real Relationships
   Don't fake it. People can smell phony care. If you want to challenge someone directly, they need to know you give a damn about them. State the facts and don't sugarcoat the concerns.

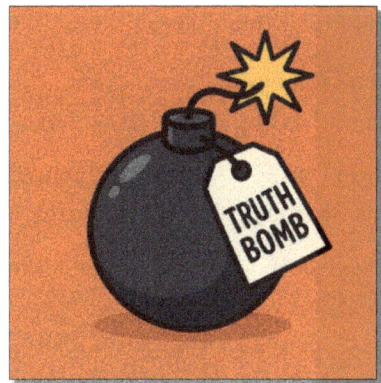

2. Give Feedback Immediately and Respectfully
    The best feedback is fast, private, specific, and comes from a place of wanting the other person to succeed. Focus on behaviours or actions, not the person.
    Say things like, "This isn't your best work, and I know you can do better," or "We missed the mark here. Let's figure out how to fix it together."
    Pay attention to how the recipient is responding.

3. Ask for Feedback, Then Actually Listen
    Start with: "What's one thing I could do better?" And then shut up. Don't justify. Don't explain. Just listen and thank them.

4. Don't Weaponize It
    Candor without care is cruelty. This isn't your license to unload. If you can't say it with respect, wait until you can.

When Radical Candor Goes Sideways

This isn't a magic bullet, and it can go wrong. Sometimes people confuse honesty with bluntness and forget to show they care. Others fall back into Ruinous Empathy because they hate conflict and would rather be liked than effective. Some deliver feedback inconsistently, which slowly erodes trust.

And let's be honest: if the power dynamics are off or the culture's not ready, Radical Candor can feel threatening. It takes time and intention to build the kind of trust that makes it work.

When Geoff called me a tyrant, it was a punch in the gut. But it made me stop, reflect, and eventually change.

Radical Candor is uncomfortable. But it's also freeing. It builds stronger teams, sharper execution, and much less drama.

If you've been avoiding a tough conversation, consider this your sign: say the thing. Kindly. Directly. Now.

It might be the best gift you give—or get—all year.

Original post URL: https://bradpoulos.com/radical-candor/

Stretch Goals Shouldn't Snap: The Art of Setting Performance Targets

Originally posted on July 12 2025.

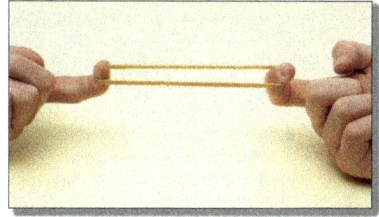

In its heyday between the 1950s and the 1980s, IBM was widely admired for its disciplined sales culture. Their salesforce was rigorously trained, methodical, and relentlessly focused on results. It had its quirks. For example, the dress code. But it worked.

One of their secret weapons was knowing how to set sales quotas at the sweet spot that's both challenging and achievable.

They'd set ambitious sales targets that were engineered to stretch people just enough to push performance without undermining morale or triggering burnout.

This stands in sharp contrast to the reality of today. In 2023, Forrester reported that approximately half of sales reps in B2B hit their quota. A healthy attainment rate is closer to 75-80%. It really is a balancing act. If 90% of your sales representatives are meeting quota, then you likely don't have truly stretch goals. And that might be fine for your business and the way you've set up your sales compensation.

I like to think of sales or other targets like a rubber band. You can stretch them, but only so far before they snap. When a goal has the right amount of stretch, it generates energy and focus. But when goals are pushed beyond what people believe is possible, motivation gives way to frustration, and eventually to disengagement. The art is in the tension.

The Psychology of Goal Commitment

In 1990, psychologists Edwin Locke and Gary Latham published what's now a foundational idea in goal-setting theory:

> *"If individuals perceive that they are unlikely to attain the goal, they are less likely to commit and therefore less likely to exert effort."*
>
> – Locke and Latham

In other words, belief matters as much as ambition. A goal that feels possible pulls effort and energy toward it. But when a goal feels out of reach, people don't just try and fail; they disengage entirely, and don't give much thought to how much they're going to fail by. Effort doesn't taper off; it falls off a cliff. The human brain simply checks out when it doesn't believe success is on the table. This is why perceived attainability is a core ingredient in any effective goal. Without it, even talented, motivated people will stop trying long before the deadline arrives.

This dynamic isn't limited to sales. Whether it's a product launch deadline, a customer satisfaction metric, or a cost-cutting target, the same psychological effect applies. When a goal feels unattainable, people stop pushing. They give up, prioritizing other work they can win at.

When Stretch Goals Snap

Get this wrong, and what you hoped would be inspiration instead creates demoralization and then apathy. Quiet quitting results in a purely performative effort. And it can be contagious. Just watch what happens if you tolerate people going through the motions without real drive!

In sales environments, you'll see salespeople who check out on their quota start sandbagging (delaying deals until the next period to improve their chances of hitting future targets or qualifying for bonuses).

This affects cash flow, throws off forecasts, and normalizes a toxic culture of disinformation.

It's particularly insidious that not only do people stop caring about hitting the target, but they stop caring about even coming close. Once belief in the goal evaporates, so does the effort.

Calibrating Your Targets

How do you create the kind of stretch that inspires without breaking people?

Inclusion. Involve your team in setting the goals. Buy-in matters.

Objectivity. Use data, not wishful thinking, as your foundation.

Incrementalism. Design incentives that reward progress, not just perfection. Leave room for upside, but don't punish those who fall short of a high bar. Avoid an all-or-nothing kind of plan.

Have you set overly easy or outlandish goals for your team? Set achievable, stretch goals and they might well surprise you!

Original post URL: https://bradpoulos.com/stretch-goals/

Trust Your Gut

Originally posted on July 22 2025.

When Intuition Pays Off—and the Crowd Finally Catches Up

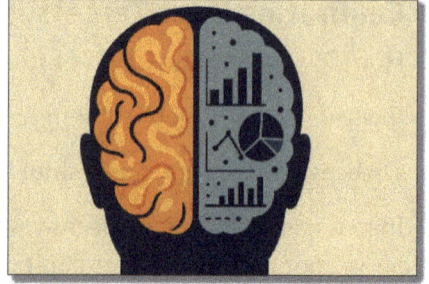

More than once in my career, I've found myself the lone voice questioning what appeared to be the conventional industry wisdom. I remember questioning Motorola's judgment when they launched Iridium. The whole industry drank their Kool-Aid, but I wasn't convinced the business model made sense. Not long after, they filed for Chapter 11 bankruptcy, a mere nine months after launching. It was one of the largest U.S. bankruptcies of its time.

Around the same time, our industry was promoting a technology called WiMAX as a competitor to mobile standards like LTE. Friends, suppliers, and competitors were excited about the prospect of a "WiMAX chip in every laptop", but I didn't believe that this more expensive technology could upset the natural upgrade path that was already underway. In the end, my skepticism was borne out, and by the mid-2010s, most WiMAX networks had either been shut down or converted to cellular technology.

More recently, in the buildup to cannabis legalization in Canada prior to 2018, I was the only person I knew who thought the numbers didn't add up. At the time, eighteen months before legalization, there were 128 licensed competitors growing weed. These companies were all touting a dubious measure called "funded capacity" (basically a measure of how much pot they could grow when fully built out), because they had no other good news to report for the billions of dollars in capital they raised. Five minutes of napkin math told me that it would only take the two largest companies in the industry to satisfy all the demand for weed in the country once they fully built out their plant. I was left wondering who the other 126 players would be selling to. It was brutally obvious to me that this industry was headed for a brick wall; yet, all the stocks continued to climb during that era.

In each case, there were good logical reasons for me to hold my opinion, but it was my gut that told me I was right and to go against the grain.

What exactly is trusting your gut? When should you trust it? When should you let the crowd sway you, despite what the evidence says?

What is Gut Instinct, Really?

Gut instinct isn't magic. It's usually your brain quietly connecting dots you don't even realize you've seen before. It's a kind of subconscious pattern recognition—something we humans are uniquely gifted at—built over years of experience and exposure, and millennia of evolution. When something feels off, or an opportunity just "clicks," it's often because your mind is matching what's in front of you with a mental library of similar situations.

Psychologist Gary Klein called this the *Recognition-Primed Decision Model*. He studied firefighters, soldiers, and other professionals making fast, high-stakes decisions and found they didn't consciously weigh options. Somehow, they just knew. Nobel laureate Herbert Simon summed it up well: "Intuition is nothing more and nothing less than recognition."

So when someone says, "I just knew," what they often mean is that their brain picked up on patterns their conscious mind hadn't caught yet.

Does Gut Get Better With Age and Experience?

It's tempting to think that intuition automatically improves with age. In some ways, it does. More years means more experiences, more patterns absorbed, more mental reps completed. But age alone isn't enough and can be a double-edged sword. Experience often brings overconfidence, blind spots, and ingrained, often unconscious, biases.

Researchers like Nobel laureate Daniel Kahneman point out that gut instinct only works reliably in what they call high-validity environments, or fields where decisions are followed by quick, clear feedback. Think of a firefighter who can immediately see whether a door opened the right way, or a surgeon who knows if a cut went as planned. Their instincts get reinforced, refined, or corrected in real-time.

By contrast, in more ambiguous settings (think investing, strategy, or hiring), it might take months or years to determine whether you made the right call. That delay makes it hard for your intuition to calibrate effectively. So in those environments, relying on gut instinct alone is far riskier.

So it's not age that sharpens your gut, but reflective experience. You only get better if you've been paying attention to what worked, what didn't, and why.

Gut vs. Structured Decision-Making

It's important not to assume a false dichotomy here. Intuition and analysis each have their place in the decision-making process. The sweet spot is knowing how to use *both.*

Your gut shines in fast-moving or human-centred situations: when you're under time pressure, when you recognize a familiar scenario, or when you're assessing intangibles like team dynamics, cultural fit, or early product-market signals. These are often situations where nuance and judgment matter more than deep analysis.

Structure, on the other hand, is critical when the stakes are high, the variables are many, or the terrain is unfamiliar. If you're making a decision that involves significant risk or long-term impact—especially in areas where you lack direct experience—you're better off gathering data, getting input from others, and relying less on intuition.

The best way to describe the way I've used this "tool" is to first let your gut surface the insight, and then use structured thinking to test it.

> *Intuition is the use of patterns they've already learned, whereas insight is the discovery of new patterns."*
> *– Gary Klein, The Power of Intuition: How to Use Your Gut Feelings to Make Better Decisions at Work*

How to Hone a Reliable Gut

Start with humility. You need to be deliberate about learning from your own decisions. That starts with running postmortems. Was your instinct correct? Either way, why? What did you see that others didn't? Or what blinded you? How much was luck a factor in this scenario?

Next, work on identifying your biases. Everyone has them, and they often come from past trauma, ego, or unchallenged assumptions. For example, if you once hired a founder-type personality who wowed everyone in meetings but couldn't deliver results, you might find yourself overly skeptical of future candidates with similar energy, even when they come with a proven track record. That's a bias, not a reasoned judgment. The better you get at spotting those mental shortcuts, the better you'll be at minimizing their impact.

It's also critical not to confuse confidence with clarity. Just because a decision feels certain doesn't mean it's sound. Confidence should follow from evidence and results, not from your planning assumptions. For instance, you might feel confident about entering a new market because the forecasts are glowing and everyone seems on board, and someone else did it somewhere else. But if your projections rest on shaky assumptions or groupthink, that confidence will bite you. Challenge your assumptions and ground your decisions in hard evidence, wherever you can.

Surround yourself with people who'll challenge you. Your instinct sharpens when it's stress-tested by thoughtful disagreement, not just confirmation. Avoid what I call "The Emperor's New Clothes Syndrome," where the higher-ups aren't challenged by those in the lower ranks, even when they all know they're making mistakes. To counter this, build a culture that rewards honest dissent and encourages respectful pushback. Encourage Radical Candor.

Lastly, keep exposing yourself to new experiences. The more patterns you take in, the richer your intuitive database becomes. Even better if these experiences are across industries, cultures, and contexts. Nothing sharpens instinct like being thrown into situations where the rules are different and you have to make sense of them from scratch.

What makes intuition powerful is drawing on this rich internal database of lived experience and observation. And when it's sharpened through honest reflection, constructive challenge, and wide exposure, it becomes a vital tool for the small business owner.

Original post URL: https://bradpoulos.com/business-intuition/

We Are What We Repeatedly Do

Originally posted on August 19 2025.

The famous words of the title were first uttered by Aristotle millennia ago. He nailed it.

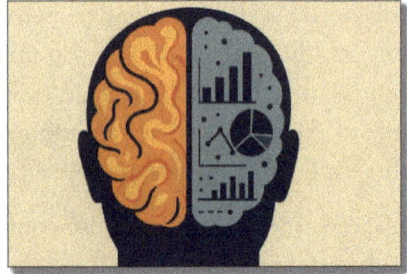

And 18th-century writer Samuel Johnson laid it on even thicker:

> *"The chains of habit are too light to be felt until they are too heavy to be broken."*

The imagery is powerful: habit as a chain. At first, it's weightless, invisible, almost harmless. But link by link, repetition forges strength. Before long, what once felt optional becomes binding.

The Power of Repetition

At its core, this is a lesson about the silent power of repetition. Habits, good or bad, form in the background of our lives, long before we realize they're defining us.

Start by working outward from a base of fundamentals like good sleep, regular and vigorous exercise, healthy food and a spiritual practice. Those disciplined enough to maintain such positive fundamentals and use alcohol and other substances moderately create the energy, clarity, and resilience they need for everything else. From there, discipline in daily routines, consistent effort in our craft, and deliberate choices in how we spend our time all stack up into the person we are.

Positive habits may seem small and forgettable in the short run. Over time, they compound into expertise, discipline, and confidence. Negative habits work the same way in the opposite direction. Ignore health, delay tough conversations, or rely on shortcuts often enough, and eventually the chain is too heavy to shake.

To round out the triumvirate of quotes to drive the point home:

> *At 20, you have the face you were born with; at 40, you*
> *have the face life gives you; and at 50, you have the face you*
> *deserve.*
> *– George Orwell, with help from Coco Chanel*

Organizational Scale Habits

For individuals, habits are our personal foundation. Companies can also form habits, with systems!

A business isn't just the sum of its big decisions; it's the outcome of repeated patterns.

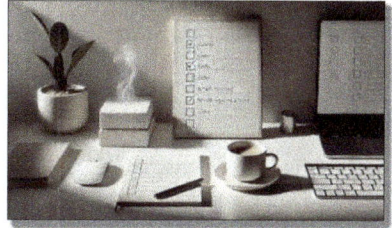

Weak systems create bad habits at scale: underpricing over and over again, waiting until tax season to look at numbers, or relying on one person to hold all the know-how. They don't feel like emergencies at first, but over time they lock the organization into fragility.

Strong systems do the opposite. Weekly cash-flow reviews, consistent processes for onboarding, or a rhythm of customer check-ins all become "organizational habits." Over the years, these invisible routines compound into durable strength.

Breaking or Building Chains

The lesson is simple, but not easy: pay attention while the links are still light.

If you want to break a bad habit, catch it while it's just a pattern—still easy to disrupt. If you want to build a good one, don't dismiss small acts: five minutes planning your day, one healthy meal, one workout, one focused deep-work session. Each link matters.

And for your business: ask what systems you're reinforcing each week. Are they the kind that silently erode you, or the kind that anchor you to growth?

Original post URL: https://bradpoulos.com/importance-of-habits/

Playing Dumb

Originally posted on August 23 2025.

A Tool For the Smartest People

Evolution has conditioned us to follow the
smartest person in the room. Our survival depended on following those who
could find food, remember safe routes, or solve new problems. Although they
weren't teaching it yet, signalling theory was alive and well in the Stone Age.
Intelligence signalled competence; competence meant survival.

Today, the signals we're most likely to follow are the gift of the gab, the ability
to dazzle with jargon, or always having the quick answer. People with natural
charisma, or the ability to hold court and defend an argument with aplomb,
have a leg up on others if their ambition is to lead.

What's less obvious is that the really smart ones know when to look confused
or even a little clueless, because sometimes "playing dumb" is the smartest
move you can make.

This doesn't mean faking ignorance in every situation. There are times when
you absolutely need to be sharp, confident, and obviously in control. If you
are pitching investors, securing a first order from an important prospective
customer, or leading your team through a crisis, you need to be on your game
and show it. But in the thousands of lower-stakes moments where your
credibility isn't on trial, acting a little less brilliant can unlock advantages you
don't get by flexing your IQ.

Why Playing Dumb Works

Looking less sharp is actually a strategic advantage. Law 21 in Robert Greene's
somewhat controversial book, *The 48 Laws of Power,* notes:

> *Given how important the idea of intelligence is to most
> people's vanity, it is critical never inadvertently to insult or
> impugn a person's brain power. That is an unforgivable sin.
> But if you can make this iron rule work for you, it opens up
> all sorts of avenues of deception. Subliminally reassure people*

> *that they are more intelligent than you are, or even that you*
> *are a bit of a moron, and you can run rings around them.*
> *The feeling of intellectual superiority you give them will*
> *disarm their suspicion-muscles."*

There are several mechanisms at play when you play dumb:

1. Information Gathering
   When you ask a basic or "naïve" question, others often over-explain. In the process, they give away details they wouldn't share with someone they see as a rival or threat.

2. Ego Management
   Everyone likes to feel like the expert. If you rush to prove how much you know, you rob others of that satisfaction. By holding back, you make people feel valued, while you gather insights.

3. De-escalation
   If a situation is heated, looking a bit clueless can cool things down. It signals you're not there to fight, which often makes the other side soften.

4. Strategic Underestimation
   Competitors, colleagues, even customers are less guarded if they don't see you as a big threat. Being underestimated can be an edge, because you're operating with more room than they realize.

This isn't a universal tool.

Play clueless when you need information, leverage, or space to move; play smart when you need to earn trust and show competence. In a pitch meeting or job interview, you need authority. If you have been hired for your knowledge, they expect you to provide answers.

And obviously don't overdo it. If you lay it on too thick, you risk looking insincere or manipulative.

Nobody Embodied This Better Than Lt. Columbo.

The lovable 1970s TV detective, Lt. Columbo put on a masterclass in this art. He shuffled around in his rumpled trench coat, always scratching his head and saying, "Oh, just one more thing..." To the suspects, he seemed bumbling, forgetful, maybe even slow.

But it was all an act. Columbo's apparent cluelessness disarmed them, made them overconfident, and got them talking. [The book has a whole chapter on this. See page 210.]

Other examples of the clueless act are Tyrion Lannister from Game of Thrones, who often allowed others to underestimate him because of his stature and wit, the crafty Odysseus, who'd feign madness or weakness to outwit his enemies, and Tom Sawyer who shrewdly persuaded the local brood to pay him for the "privilege" of painting a fence.

The Real Genius

Playing clueless is not about faking it. It's about control. The smartest people know they don't need to look brilliant at every turn. They know when to sit back, let others reveal themselves, and keep their aces hidden until the right moment.

Sometimes, the smartest move is to let others think you don't have one.

Original post URL: https://bradpoulos.com/playing-dumb/

Good Enough Might Be Great

Originally posted on September 13 2025.

How to Make Faster, Smarter Decisions in Business

Most small business owners believe they need to get every decision right. The best software. The best supplier. The best marketing strategy.

But here's the trap: chasing the "best" often drains your time, energy, and momentum.

The good news? You don't need the perfect answer. You need a good-enough one that keeps you moving. That's the essence of a powerful mental model for entrepreneurs: satisficing vs. maximizing. For those 80% of times when perfect is the enemy of good (enough).

The Psychology of Decision Fatigue

Picture this. You spend three weeks comparing email marketing tools. You devour reviews, build spreadsheets, binge YouTube tutorials. Finally, you pick one... and barely use it.

That's maximizing: the drive to find the single, absolute best choice. Maximizers believe there must be a "right" answer, so they keep hunting, even when it costs them more than it pays back.

Satisficers, on the other hand, define their criteria, choose a solution that meets it, and stop searching. They optimize for movement, not perfection. It's the difference between spending 20 minutes picking a shirt versus scanning your closet, grabbing the first one that works, and getting on with your day.

As a founder, you make dozens if not hundreds of decisions a week. Maximize all of them, and you'll burn out. The key skill is knowing which decisions deserve that level of scrutiny and which don't.

Maximizing Hurts Small Business Owners

Maximizing feels responsible, but it comes with hidden costs:

- Time cost: Hours lost comparing instead of building.
- Opportunity cost: Every delayed decision slows results.
- Mental cost: Fatigue builds until you avoid decisions altogether.
- Execution risk: By the time you choose, the window may have closed— or your team has moved on.

In business, there usually isn't a single "best" answer. There are multiple good options, and most of them can work—if you commit.

The 80/20 Rule of Decision-Making

So when should you maximize? A simple rule of thumb: maximize the 20% of decisions that drive 80% of your outcomes. Satisfice the rest. Here's how that might look in practice. Satisfice on:

- Software tools
- Invoice templates
- Business cards, logos, branding frills
- Scheduling systems
- Early admin hires

Maximize on:

- Pricing model or business model
- Market positioning
- Choice of business partner
- Legal structure
- Key sales hires

Not everything deserves your obsession. Save it for the choices that truly shape your business.

Case Study: The CRM That Never Got Used

A new client of mine had just spent months agonizing over which CRM to buy. She compared HubSpot, Zoho, and half a dozen others. Built spreadsheets. Ran demos. Consulted mentors.

Eventually, she chose what looked best on paper.

But the team hated it. They never adopted it. Six months later, they scrapped it for something simpler they actually used.

Had she defined success as "a tool my team will use within the first week" and made a faster call, she would've saved months of wasted time and frustration.

When Maximizing Makes Sense

Satisficing isn't sloppiness. Some decisions deserve maximizing effort.

Maximize when:

- The decision is irreversible
- It has serious legal or compliance implications
- It's strategically central to your value proposition or customer experience

These are your "80/20" decisions. They're the ones where the cost of being wrong is truly high. Luckily, most decisions don't fall into this category.

The Takeaway

You're not building a perfect business—you're building a working one.

Progress, not perfection, is what scales. The entrepreneurs who win aren't the ones who maximize every choice. They're the ones who keep choosing, quickly and consistently.

Satisficing isn't settling. It's strategy. Good enough might just be great.

Original post URL: https://bradpoulos.com/satisficing

A Bias Toward Action

Originally posted on October 11 2025

At a university, a professor asked his students: "If there are four birds on a tree and three of them decided to fly away, how many are left on the tree?" Everyone answered, "One." They were surprised when one student disagreed and said, "Four birds remain." This caught everyone's attention.

The professor asked him: "How so?"

He replied: "You said they decided to fly, but you didn't say they actually flew. Making a decision doesn't mean taking action."

It's a teaching story that circulates widely, and for good reason. Decision doesn't equal action. A bias toward action is one of my personal fundamental values. I don't want to leave the earth regretting what I "coulda, woulda and shoulda". I tell my students I'd rather regret that I did something than regret that I didn't.

The Small Business Reality

In small business, the gap between decision and action kills more dreams than bad ideas ever will. I've seen it several times over the years. The otherwise savvy entrepreneur who "decided" six months ago that their culture-poisoning sales manager Stuart should be fired, but repeatedly postpones the action. The pricing increase that's been "decided" since Q1 but somehow the old rates keep getting quoted. The bad client everyone knows needs to go but keeps getting one more chance.

This matters more in small business than in corporate life. You don't have bureaucracy to blame, or scale to absorb waste. Resources are tight, which means indecision is expensive. Every month you don't raise prices means profits foregone forever. Speed is supposed to be your competitive advantage over bigger players. Don't squander that advantage by overthinking.

I'm not condoning recklessness or impulsivity, but rather a clear-eyed recognition that in business the cost of indecision often exceeds the cost of a wrong decision. Most bets are small, so act that way.

Why We Get Stuck

The psychological barriers are real. Fear of irreversibility stops us cold. What if I regret firing Stuart, raising prices, or cutting that service? Perfectionism whispers that we should wait for the perfect moment, the perfect plan, or the perfect conditions. Decision fatigue compounds everything. When you're making a hundred small decisions daily, the big ones get endlessly postponed.

But here's the truth that nearly twenty years of teaching and consulting has taught me: Most business decisions are more reversible than we think. You can re-hire, adjust pricing, bring back a service. Coca-Cola's introduction of New Coke in the 1980s is a great example. They replaced Classic Coke, met a massive backlash, and reversed the decision within months.

Even at their scale, the decision turned out to be reversible. The "perfect moment" doesn't exist—there's just "now" and "too late." And small businesses die from inaction far more often than from wrong action. The key insight is understanding the difference between strategic patience and procrastination. Strategic patience means waiting for the right information, doing due diligence on a major investment, or testing a market before scaling. Procrastination is avoiding discomfort.

Often, what we call "being careful" is procrastination dressed up in business language. Perfectionism can also lead to decision delay. Consider Colin Powell's "40-70 rule" which states that you need between 40 and 70 per cent of the total information to make a decision. With less than 40 per cent, you will likely make a poor choice, and with more than 70 per cent, you will end up taking too long, and the decision will be made for you!

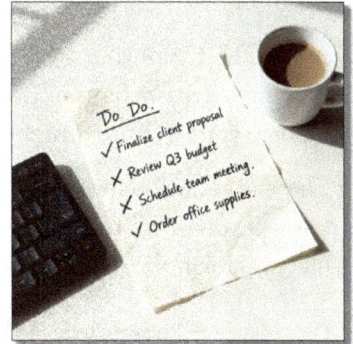

What Action Actually Looks Like

So what does a bias toward action look like in practice?

Here are real decisions small business owners face, and what action (not just deciding) actually means:

The Personnel Problem

DECIDED: "Stuart needs to go. He's toxic, underperforming, or just the wrong fit."

ACTION: Start documentation today. Pull his file and review performance issues tonight. Review the employment agreement to understand your obligations. Book a meeting with your lawyer or HR consultant this week. Have the conversation next week. Not next quarter when it's "less busy".

Stuart is costing you money and morale every single day.

The Pricing Decision

DECIDED: "We're underpriced by 15%. Everyone tells us our quality is worth more."

ACTION: Email your next three prospects with the new rates today. Send existing clients written notice with a 90-day grandfather period this week. Update your website tonight. No more discounting because you're nervous.

The market will tell you if you're wrong, and you can adjust. But you'll never know if you don't test it. If you're wondering what the impact of the price increase might be, check out this article.

Or, on a more personal note...

you've DECIDED: "I need to lose these 30 lbs that crept up on me these last five years."

ACTION: Sign up for the gym again today. Start eating better with the very next meal, not next week. Restrict alcohol to the weekends starting right now, not "after tomorrow's beer league game".

If your health matters, it matters now. Action has a today or a this week component. Specificity. Small, irreversible steps that create momentum. Once you've sent the email, cancelled the subscription, or booked the appointment, momentum can take over.

The Action Bias Framework

To make this easier at first, time-box your decisions. Give yourself a deadline. "I'll decide about hiring/firing/pricing by Friday at noon." Then honour it.

The decision doesn't get better by aging like wine. Create a personal bias toward reversible actions. Most decisions can be undone or adjusted. The ones that truly can't like selling the company, taking on a business partner, or signing a 10-year lease deserve considerable deliberation. But most others are completely reversible.

The Entrepreneur's Advantage

Speed of execution is the small business superpower. It's your advantage over the corporate giants with their committees and approval processes. When you squander that advantage by acting like you need consensus from people who don't exist, you're giving away the only structural advantage you have. The birds that decide and fly are the ones that survive. The ones that just decide? They're still sitting on the branch when winter comes, cold and getting hungry.

Original post URL: https://bradpoulos.com/bias-toward-action/

Forget Money. Here's What Really Motivates People

Originally posted on October 21 2025

Understanding Herzberg's Motivation-Hygiene Theory

Ever tried to boost team morale with a small raise or a pizza lunch and found the effects short-lived? Or given someone a raise only to see their performance drop off? Many small business owners confuse what keeps employees satisfied with what simply keeps them from quitting. We throw money at problems, celebrate birthdays with cake, upgrade the break room coffee, and wonder why people still seem disengaged or, worse, start looking elsewhere.

The truth is, we're often solving the wrong problem entirely. As my dad would say:

> *Son, you've got the em-PHA-sis on the wrong syl-LA-ble!*
> *- The late James Poulos (Brad's Dad)*

Frederick Herzberg's Motivation-Hygiene Theory (also called the "Two-Factor Theory") helps you put that em-PHA-sis where it belongs. This durable framework will change how you think about managing people, which is crucial when employee engagement is at all time lows.

Two Buckets: Hygiene Factors vs. Motivators

Herzberg's theory, developed in the 1950s after interviewing thousands of workers, is eye-opening. It splits job factors into two distinct categories that we often think of as opposites, but are really on completely separate tracks.

Hygiene factors are the first bucket. These don't necessarily make people love their jobs, but if they're missing, you'll absolutely hear about it. Think of them as the baseline, the cost of entry, or the stuff that has to be right or everything can fall apart. These factors, when you get them wrong, will lead directly to job dissatisfaction.

But the counterintuitive part is that when you get them right, you don't get real satisfaction, you just get an absence of dissatisfaction. In other words they can be at best neutral in their effect on employee performance or engagement. Getting them wrong will sting you but getting them right doesn't bring any huge reward for the company.

The other surprising thing is that hygiene factors include salary and benefits. Others, like company policies that actually make sense, decent working conditions, job security, quality supervision, and functional relationships with co-workers are also important to get right, but keep in mind that none of these are motivational. The hygiene factors get you to neutral, at best. You can pay someone well, give them great benefits, and have a fair scheduling policy, and they will not necessarily feel motivated. They keep people from actively hating their jobs and not quitting, but that's about it.

Motivators, the second bucket, are where things get interesting. These factors make people feel genuinely fulfilled and motivated to do their best work. We're talking about recognition for accomplishments, a sense of achievement, opportunities for personal growth, increased responsibility, finding meaning in the work itself, and clear paths for advancement.

These are the things that make people say "I love my job" instead of just "my job is fine." And here's the crucial part: you can't substitute one bucket for the other. You can't fix a lack of recognition by bumping someone's salary by two percent. It doesn't work that way. You have to actively manage the elements in both buckets.

The Money Paradox

Here's where it gets tricky, and where a lot of business owners get confused: money is not a motivator, but the promise of money can be.

Your current salary, no matter how generous, becomes what you feel you're worth. It's the baseline. You'll give a good day's work for a good day's pay, but that steady paycheck won't make you go the extra mile. Once it hits your bank account, it's a hygiene factor. Necessary, but not motivating.

Raises too. They lose their motivational power quickly. The day after you get it you're walking on air, but by the time the first paycheque comes the extra money is matched to expectations.

But a bonus tied to hitting a specific goal is different. The promise of future money, contingent on achievement, can absolutely motivate. Commissions, profit-sharing, or performance bonuses are always out there; always something to work toward. And the more meaningful they are to an employee's overall compensation, that is, the greater proportion they make up, the more meaningfully they will shape behaviour.

The downside is that the concept works in both directions. The promise of money can be motivating. And the promise of NO money will sap that motivation. If a salesperson tops out their bonus by Halloween, they're apt to sandbag until January to help pad next year's sales, and increase the chances of maxing out again.

People will always behave in the way that the systems you create influence them to. If you want your salespeople to keep selling all year, and maybe even work harder in the final stretches, create a progressive compensation system; don't design in reasons for people to stop working.

Why It Matters to Small Business Owners

This distinction is especially important for those of us running small businesses. We often can't compete with larger firms when it comes to pay or perks. We're not offering six-figure salaries, a comprehensive retirement plan, or fancy corporate retreats in Cabo.

Our superpower is that we can offer work that actually matters, real responsibility that isn't buried under seven layers of corporate bureaucracy, and a strong sense of how an individual contribution is moving the needle. In a small business, people can see the direct impact of their work. They're not just a cog in a massive machine. This can bring a powerful sense of belonging that motivates and retains the right people.

The employees who thrive in small businesses are not usually the ones chasing the biggest paycheque. They're the ones who want autonomy, who want to grow, who want to feel like what they do matters. Those are motivator-driven people, and that's your competitive advantage.

And the kicker is that it doesn't cost anything, really, to create the culture and systems that support motivators. At least nothing close to a trip to Cabo!

Putting Two-Factor Theory Into Practice

You have a shop-floor employee who complains about inconsistent schedules. One week they're opening, the next they're closing, and they never know what's coming. That's a hygiene issue. It's about working conditions and company policies. Fixing it might stop them from quitting, and you absolutely should fix it, but doing so won't make them love the job. They'll just stop being actively annoyed about their schedule.

But what if you take a different approach? What if you start involving them in workflow decisions, asking for their input on how to improve efficiency or solve recurring problems? What if you offer a clear path to becoming a floor supervisor, with increasing responsibility along the way? What if you even gave the staff input into the schedule? Now that's a motivator. Now they're not just showing up and watching the clock. They're engaged. They're thinking about the business when they're not at work. They're bringing ideas to the table.

Same employee, completely different outcome.

Get the Basics Right, Then Aim Higher

Think of hygiene factors as the foundation of a house. Get them wrong, and nothing else matters. You can't build a beautiful home on a cracked foundation. If people don't feel they're paid fairly, if your policies are chaotic, if the work environment is toxic, none of your recognition programs or growth opportunities will land.

But a solid foundation alone doesn't make a house inspiring. Once the hygiene factors are optimized you need to focus on the motivators. That's where you build something special.

The small businesses that punch above their weight—the ones with loyal, engaged teams despite not having corporate budgets—are the ones that understand this distinction. They get the little things right, AND they invest heavily in making work meaningful, developing their people, and giving them real ownership and recognition.

Original post URL: https://bradpoulos.com/motivation

Don't Follow Your Passion — Follow Your Talent Instead

Originally posted on November 15 2025

When I was a kid, I didn't really have any passions perhaps beyond hockey, and while I dreamed of it, I was never delusional enough to think I'd make the NHL. I didn't have a single burning interest that guided my choices. I wasn't a born doctor or dream chef. I stumbled into work the way most people do: by accident.

I started in the jewellery business as an extension of my part-time job in high school, got bored around age 22, and then went to tech school for the sole reason that my brother was already enrolled, and it seemed like an ok idea to move to Toronto and do that. There was no grand plan. No following of passion. My first job was equally opportunistic and lacking in any strategic justification.

And that's precisely the point. We've been sold a fantasy that career success starts with passion. Find what you love, and the money will follow.

I mean, can these people be wrong?

> *"Follow your passion. Do what you love, and the money will follow. Most people don't believe it, but it's true."*
> *- Oprah Winfrey*

> *"In the world of business, the people who are most successful are those who are doing what they love."*
> *- Warren Buffett*

> *"Don't aim for success if you want it; just do what you love*
> *and believe in, and it will come naturally."*
> *- David Frost (British TV personality)*

What they don't mention is that only 2% of professional actors make a living from their craft without supplementary employment. Chasing success by following your passion is more likely to spoil it, turning it into a thing you do for (little) money, but no longer love.

The Great Passion Lie

"Follow your passion" is the feel-good lie of modern work culture. It sounds empowering, but as Scott Galloway says, it's "advice from the already rich."

The people telling you to follow your passion often made their fortune in unglamorous fields, then they turn around and tell others to chase their bliss. The irony is that most people, like yours truly at age 20+, can't identify a single passion to follow. Some 2008 research by Stanford psychologist William Damon found that only 20% of people under 26 can articulate one.

Even when people do have a passion, it's usually something creative like acting, music, or design. These fields are brutally competitive and financially unforgiving.

Follow Your Talent, and Passion Will Follow

Talent is observable and testable. You can measure progress, earn feedback, and build momentum. When you get good at something, recognition and rewards follow, and you're very likely to gain passion as a result of your success.

Very few people dream of being a high-value software salesperson, or the VP of Operations at an energy company, but when you get to the top of these domains, life is actually very good, fueling the passion in a positive feedback loop.

As Galloway says, "Mastery begets passion. Success creates enthusiasm. Economic security multiplies options."

Mark Cuban Agrees

Cuban puts it bluntly, "No. Follow your effort. No one quits anything they're good at. If I followed my passion, I'd still be trying to play professional basketball."

Cuban's point is that passion follows excellence. When you invest consistent effort in something you do well, the resulting success and mastery ignite passion.

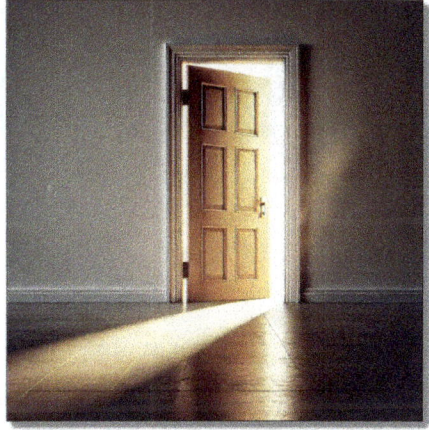

Cal Newport, author of *So Good They Can't Ignore You*, backs this up with research. He found no evidence that matching your job to a pre-existing passion makes people happier or more successful. What actually leads to satisfaction at work are three factors:

- Autonomy: Control over what you do and when
- Mastery: The pursuit of excellence
- Relationships: Working with people you respect

Notice that none of these depend on starting with passion. In fact I've got a whole article on what makes for satisfied employees (Index: motivation).

The Contrarian Nuance

Not everyone dismisses passion entirely. Some argue we've misunderstood it. The word comes from the Latin *pati*, meaning *to suffer*. Real passion isn't just enthusiasm. It's what you're willing to endure hardship for. That kind of passion emerges from deep commitment, not from chasing excitement. Like what it takes to become a virtuoso, or an elite athlete.

And for some, passion doesn't have to come from their career at all. Your work might fund your passion. You don't have to love the business if it gives you the life you love.

Why Passion Is Dangerous for Entrepreneurs

For entrepreneurs, passion can be blinding. It gives false confidence and leads people to ignore fundamentals like margins, market demand, and scale.

If you love coffee, that doesn't mean you should open a café. If you're obsessed with fashion, that doesn't mean a boutique is the right move. The graveyard of failed startups is littered with people who loved their idea more than their customers did. I read this 30 years ago in The *E-Myth* by Michael Gerber. Passion will cause you to think more about working in the business than on the business.

Instead of asking, "What am I passionate about?" ask:

- What am I good at that others value?
- Where can I achieve mastery faster than competitors?
- What problems can I solve profitably and repeatedly?

Sustainable businesses live in the overlap of skill, value, and demand.

A Better Way to Think About Passion

Here's the paradox: passion does matter, but as a result, not a starting point. Once you achieve competence and confidence in a particular area, the work itself becomes rewarding. Passion is what mastery feels like on the inside.

In my own career, I've experienced seasons of boredom and burnout, but also flashes of deep engagement that only came after I became proficient in something. Teaching, consulting, and writing all grew out of skills I built first. The passion came later, as a byproduct of mastery.

Passion is a reward

"Follow your passion" sounds romantic, but it's hollow. It lets you feel purposeful without making the hard choices. The people who build meaningful, prosperous careers do it by following talent, effort, and opportunity.

Get so good they can't ignore you. Passion will show up right about the time the invoices start getting paid.

Original post URL: https://bradpoulos.com/dont-follow-your-passion

MANAGEMENT & STRATEGY

What is The Right Way to Fire Someone

Originally posted on February 16, 2021

There's a Right Way to Fire Someone... and it's a lot simpler than you think

I have a couple of "rules" around the right way to fire someone, but it's mostly about keeping it short and simple.

For starters, no one should ever be surprised that they're being fired. If that happens, you suck as a manager. Firing should be the final arrow in your quiver. In some future post I will discuss everything that leads up to this point, and of course that advice will vary by jurisdiction since my readers in the UK, US, Canada and Australia are all dealing with different labour laws. In some cases, terminating an employee is incredibly difficult (Ontario) and expensive and in others, it's just a matter of deciding (California).

So once you've decided to make this step and assuming you care about the right way to fire someone, there are a few must do's regardless of the local labour laws.

Set and Setting

It will all be easier if you are able to choose a location that is somewhat private (not some fishbowl conference room for example). You must have a witness. Exactly who will depend on the size of your company / branch. If there's a dedicated HR person on site, then it's them. If not, choose a neutral party, preferably at a level or two above the person being terminated. You should be planning to have the employee leave immediately. Don't allow them to convince you that they "just need to finish up x", or "really need to brief the team on y". Thank them for their concern and let them know you will be in touch if need be.

There is some debate about what day is best. My rule is not Monday or Friday. And i really do think it should be done earlier in the day, rather than at the end. Mostly because it seems kind of crappy to squeeze that last day of work out of someone.

> *The first four words you say should be "We're Letting You Go".*

Honestly. I know it's hard. But I've made the huge mistake of *not* doing it this way. Trust me the right way to fire someone is to tell them right away. Direct, Radical Candor is more humane than any other way. Literally, "[Insert Name] I asked you to meet today because we've decided that we're going to let you go" (or "terminate your employment", whatever flows off the tongue best). **Any** watering down of this initial statement will only get you in trouble. Establish at the outset that the decision is the only thing that's not negotiable. The rest (severance, references, the company car, etc.) we can talk about. But you're fired.

Be Honest about Why

In some jurisdictions (including Ontario where I live and work), you are required to be honest about the reason someone is being let go. It will be seen as bad faith dealing if you lie about it. So even if you're not letting someone go "for cause", you have to be honest about why they are being terminated.

After the meeting

How you handle things after meeting the employee is just as important as your conduct during it. Allow the Employee to maintain their dignity by letting them choose whether to remove their personal effects right away or at a later time. If they want to say goodbye, let them.

In most cases, you'll be asked for a reference. This can be tricky if the employee was a very poor performer, as an inaccurate reference could leave you open to a lawsuit. But in most cases, you'll be able to offer a reasonably-worded reference letter, and you should. Your current employees will judge you by how you treat the terminated ones. So being unreasonable about this or any other particular will lead to punishment by your staff.

Remember that the termination meeting you're about to have may very well be one of the Top 10 worst things to happen in the person on the other side of the desk's lifetime. It ranks up there with divorce or death of a loved one for many. So while Radical Candor is always the way, remember that kindness is almost always an option.

How NOT to fire someone...

Here's a short story that perfectly illustrates why you need to be very direct during that first few seconds of the meeting.

Our company had an inside salesperson, who we will call Bill, who was not getting the job done so his supervisor, a newly-minted National Sales Manager (let's call him Arthur) and I decided he should be placed on a formal Performance Improvement Program (yes, the dreaded PIP). Art had recently been promoted from a sales position, and had no formal business training. It was therefore incumbent on me to make sure he knew how to manage the meeting with Bill, and I failed abysmally. I didn't explain to Art about the first four words, laying out the non-negotiable fact that Bill was being placed on probation and that he needed to improve.

As a result, Art and Bill went down a rabbit hole and it took some time for Bill to come around to the fact that he needed to up his game. It likely took around 1/2 hour or so to finally get Bill committed to working differently, and then almost anti-climatically Art pushes a letter across the table at Bill and said something like, "so we're going to put you on a performance improvement program". Bill was stunned as he had himself convinced, with our help, that this was just a chit chat. We then had to repeat much of what had been covered, and re-convince Bill that this was in his interest. As an experience, the meeting was on par with having a tooth filled.

Had I equipped Art with the knowledge that he should start by saying something more like, "Bill, we're concerned about your performance and we'd like to talk to you about a formal program to help you get back on track", the meeting would have been half as long, and half as painful for all concerned.

Original post URL: https://bradpoulos.com/entrepreneurship/the-right-way-to-fire-someone/

Small Business Culture – Getting it Right

Originally posted on May 17, 2021.

Small Business Culture is No Accident

We've all heard about incredible businesses to work at, where people are treated as valued partners and no one wants to go home because work is much meaningful fun. Or something similar. People compete heavily to work at places like Hubspot (#1 on Glassdoor's 2020 list of top employers) or Trader Joe's (tops on Forbes' 2019 list). Companies like Zappos, Warby Parker, and Southwest Airlines are legendary for the efforts they put toward creating and reinforcing their company culture.

When thinking about how your small business culture should evolve over time, keep in mind my axioms when it comes to culture.

5. Culture doesn't happen by accident; you have to work at it.

6. A great culture can only come from great values.

7. Great companies hire for values above all else.

But is small business culture as easy to develop as in a large business? Arguably, it should be easier. After all, it's much easier to maneuver a canoe than it is an ocean liner! It's just that many don't bother to try. And that's a shame because I'm not sure it's even possible to create a great business without a foundation of a great culture.

Firespring – Small Business Culture on Steroids

One company that I admire for its ability to put these axioms into action and create a great small business culture is Firespring, a marketing firm in that hotbed of entrepreneurial activity, Lincoln, NB. Their CEO, Jay Wilkinson, has done a great job leading this company and instilling a high-performance culture while preserving a playful and interesting environment for creatives to work.

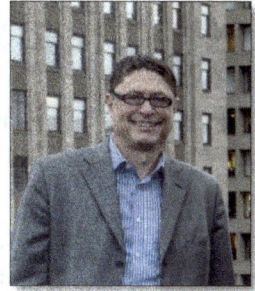

Watch Jay's 2011 TED Talk (https://youtu.be/WDFqEGI4QJ4) for tips on what you can do to emulate him.

One of the keys, according to Jay, is "hiring for values". I can't stress enough how important this is. Bad cultural fits can ruin a company.

Hiring for Values to Fashion Your Small Business Culture

When doing a second or third interview of a candidate who will report to another... it's the only thing I ever look at (since I trust my staff to make sure the candidate can do the technical part of the job before presenting them to me). I have

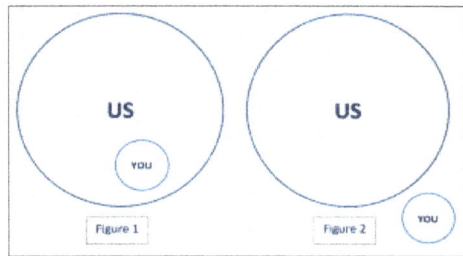

Figure 1

Figure 2

this shtick I use where I draw a circle on a piece of paper and tell them that is our corporate culture. Then I draw a circle fully inside that one (Figure 1), and another fully outside (Figure 2), and explain that it's my job to make sure that they do neither of these things to our culture.

That is, neither to fully fit in, nor to be a total outlier. My job is to make sure that they mostly fit in, but bring something new to the organization, and over time the addition of new people allows the culture to evolve naturally.

Something like in Figure 3. The reason is simple. Culture is the result of values, and values are what drive decisions in the absence of a specific policy.

Whether you're an established business or just starting out, having a deliberate culture strategy that values high performance, engagement and excellence is a necessary, but not sufficient, condition for superiority of the firm.

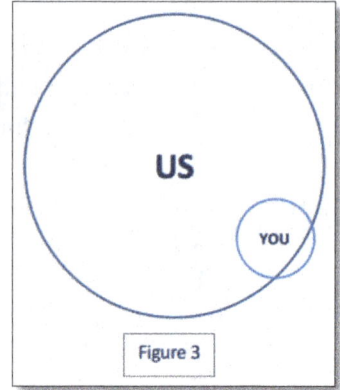

Figure 3

Original post URL: https://bradpoulos.com/small-business-culture/

Systems Thinking for Small Biz: The Case for SOPs

Originally posted on July 8, 2025.

Goals are OK. But systems rule.

I wish I could lay claim to this concept, and I'm not sure who first came up with it, but I first caught wind of it about 10 years ago when I read something by Dilbert creator Scott Adams. James Clear, author of Atomic Habits (one of the many unread books on my nightstand), also emphasizes the importance of building habits and processes rather than obsessing over outcomes.

I used to be a "goal-oriented" person. I have a list of long-term goals on a piece of paper that I've been curating for over 30 years. I've even achieved a few of them. Goals gave me direction, something to aim for. And if you're like most entrepreneurs, or if you've ever sat through an MBA course, you've been fed the gospel of goal-setting your entire professional life.

So what's the issue?

Goals don't get the work done. Systems do.

Goals are great for direction. But if you want consistent progress, reliable output, and results you can scale, you need a system.

Systems vs. Goals: What's the Real Difference?

A goal is the outcome you want.
A system is the process that gets you there.

- As a writer, my goal could be to publish a book. My system is my daily writing habit, and the Excel spreadsheet that tracks the number of words written per day (for which, incidentally, I should have a goal!).
- As a consultant, my goal might be to land five new clients this year. My system is how I nurture leads, and follow up.

- For you, the small business operator, your goal might be to free up your time. Your system is how you delegate, automate, document, and monitor.

Your goals are a snapshot of the future. They're your personal vision statement.

Systems are what you do. Kind of like a personal mission. They're biased toward action.

Why Systems Win

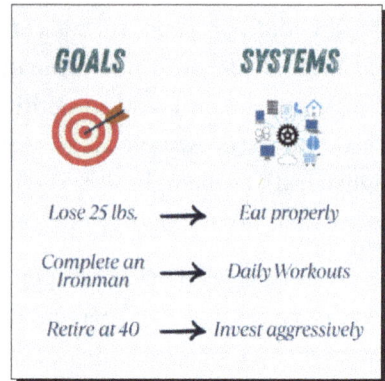

1. **Goals have a finish line. Systems keep running.**
   When you hit a goal, what happens next? Most people exhale, celebrate, and then drift. Systems, by contrast, are designed to keep going. They're built into your schedule. They become part of who you are. In the best instances, you are not even a vital part of the system. For example, you might have an automated system for onboarding new customers that includes a welcome email, automated training, a check-in call, and a satisfaction survey. And these things can scale in a way that you can't.

2. **Goals create a success/failure mindset.**
   Miss your quarterly revenue target? That's a failure. Never mind that you improved your conversion rate or shaved hours off your process. Systems reward consistency and improvement. If you show up, do the reps, and keep refining, that's progress. Hitting 98% of your profit target for the year is no "failure" in my eyes.

3. **You don't rise to the level of your goals. You fall to the level of your systems.**
   Your outcomes are trailing indicators of your systems. Good system → good outcome. Weak system → coin toss.

4. **Systems create valuable feedback loops.**
   Goals are static. You set them and then... what? Systems adapt. When something breaks, you fix the process. You learn. You tweak. That's how

you build durability into your business.

5. **What if you could only have one?**
Finally, imagine some zany world where you could only have one of either systems or goals. Which one would you choose to forego? Is a goal with no system better than a system with no goal?

But Aren't Goals Important?

Of course. They give you a heading, a rough idea of where you're going. You need SOMETHING to tell you where to point your system! But once you've got that, the focus must be on the execution of a repeatable, reliable, and efficient system.

Customers are More Important

Getting to what really matters, a customer would never pay for your goal, but they would pay for your systems. Your client does not care that you want to achieve 99% on-time delivery, but they do care that you have a built-in, reliable system with safeguards, workarounds, buffers, and contingencies to ensure timely and predictable delivery!

A System That Works

As I write this, I'm still recovering from yet another playoff loss by my Toronto Maple Leafs, again to the eventual Stanley Cup champs, the Florida Panthers, who, for the second time in a row, took out the Edmonton Oilers in the final. How Florida won it is remarkable. Every NHL team starts with the goal of winning the Cup. But Florida doesn't do it with superstars.

Their top two scorers ranked just 25th and 41st in league scoring, while their opponents included Connor McDavid, Mitch Marner, Auston Matthews, William Nylander, and Leon Draisaitl, some of the most dominant players in the game.

Paul Maurice's Panthers won with a relentless, disciplined style of play built around quick transitions, aggressive forechecking, and pressure on the puck.

Relentless buy-in from every player is elevating Florida's system-driven approach into what is starting to look like a dynasty.

You can use systems to build one of your own. The complexity can grow as you do. Start with simple things like work instructions and documented standards in a high-friction area of your business. Think about where you might add checklists, templates or other tools to increase repeatability and efficiency.

Ask yourself this:
"If I disappeared for two weeks, what would fall apart in my business?"

Whatever you just thought of, that's where you need a system!

Original post URL: https://bradpoulos.com/systems-vs-goals

Preparing Your Small Business For Recession

Originally posted on January 19, 2023.

While none of us know for sure, the signs and predictions from those in the know are that the western economies are headed for a recession. Whether that means "winter is coming" for your small business or it will just be a relatively painless, short-term slowdown is anyone's guess and not something that I'm prepared to predict.

There are several things that one should be doing to prepare, and the good news is that these are things that a savvy small business owner should be doing anyway, recession or not. My book, The Small Business Operator's Manual – A practical guide to running your small business profitably, outlines many of these in more detail.

Shore Up Customer Relationships

Losing a good customer is always somewhat painful, but to do so now could have agonizing repercussions. Spend extra time ensuring that your most valuable customer relationships are solid. Make sure your salesforce knows they're expected to have more face time, and that any customer issues are to be brought to management's attention promptly. If it's been some time since you, the owner has spent serious time on the road, visiting customers, today is the day to start.

And if you've been carrying customers that are not profitable, or are barely so, maybe now is the time to cut them loose. Note that you don't fire customers by actually firing them. You do it by raising their prices to the point that you are happy with the revenue for the amount of resources they're consuming. If they stay, at least now they're worth the trouble. If they go, you've not lost much 0f value.

Get Ruthless About Collections

Too many small business owners don't know how or won't do the work to make sure that they are paid on time. Now is the time to fix that. Anything that can be done to preserve cash flow from this point forward should be on the table, but this should be near the top of the list.

Doing regular collection calls, beginning before the due date of the invoice, and following up any stragglers quickly is one of the highest payoff moves you can make if you're trying to reduce your average collection period.

Take a Razor to Unnecessary Expenditures

It's always a good time to review where the money is going out. Don't wait for a recession to decide to cut costs and trim the fat. Do it now. This applies especially to recurring costs like subscriptions. It's often surprising how much we're spending on online services, magazines, and other services (coffee, cleaning, etc.) many of which were a great idea at the time, but since forgotten, or at least no longer as critical as they once were. You can always re-up some of these when business improves and provided that they are really needed.

Create a Cash Flow Budget

It surprises me how many clients have no budget at all, and don't plan their cash flow. Not having a cash budget is like flying a plane without instruments, and sheets over the windshield. Unless your business is flush with cash and recession-proof, you're playing with fire by not having a sharp eye on cash flow. If you're going to have a shortfall, it's much better to know that well in advance, so you can mitigate it or at least prepare for it by alerting suppliers that you might need more liberal terms, or preparing your personal life for a smaller salary.

I have always used a simple excel spreadsheet to track budgeted vs actual cash flow. If you're not sure how to set one up, my website has a template that you can download for free[3].

Carefully Consider Your Debt Situation

Many of my clients have no meaningful amount of debt and have made that decision as a personal choice to reduce stress (with the added bonus that it's literally impossible to go bankrupt if you have no debt). Others use it wisely,

---

[3] *https://bradpoulos.com/business-resources/#CashFlowPlanning*

to manage short-term dips in available cash, or to finance short-term assets like inventory and receivables.

It might seem like a good time to pay down debt, but that's going to depend on a few other factors. If the company has a bank line of credit or similar debt facility, it's likely relatively cheap money and should not be paid down unless the company has lots of cash. In fact, you might look at expanding the available cash from these sources while business is still relatively good.

Higher-interest debt may be a candidate but again it's important to balance the costs of the interest with the need to preserve cash. If in doubt, leave it alone.

The Bottom Line

While it is impossible to predict the future, it is important to take proactive steps to ensure your small business is ready for a potential recession. I learned a long time ago that transparency with key partners and other stakeholders is vital to your long-term success. In a small business, a recession doesn't need to be as painful as you may think.

Keep your employees, key suppliers, landlord, and any other stakeholders informed well ahead of any potential cash shortfalls, so that they can prepare for the worst, and your relationships will weather any short-term recessionary storms.

Taking the necessary steps now can help you prepare and protect your small business for any economic uncertainty ahead.

Original post URL: https://bradpoulos.com/small-business-strategy/small_business_recession_tips/

Small Business Strategy vs a Business Plan

Originally posted on January 19, 2023.

You've probably heard it a hundred times: "You need a business plan."

Banks say it. Consultants say it. Some well-meaning relative probably said it over dinner. And sure, if you're raising money or applying for a loan, you might need a plan to make the gatekeepers happy. But if you're like most small business owners — self-funded, customer-driven, and moving fast — you don't need a 30-page plan.

What you *do* need is a strategy.

Let's break down the difference, and why one keeps your business alive while the other mostly just eats up time and printer ink.

How do Strategy and Business Plans Differ?

A business plan is a document. A strategy is a set of choices (that you might write down in your business plan!).

- Business plans are often static, written at the beginning, and left untouched.
- Strategy is dynamic, evolving as your business grows.
- Business plans are usually written for someone else (banker, investor).
- Strategy is for YOU, to help you make decisions every damn day.

Here's a quick comparison:

Business Plan	Strategy
Long, formal, investor-facing	Short, focused, founder-facing
Emphasizes projections	Emphasizes priorities and trade-offs
Often theoretical	Grounded in real decisions
Static	Evolving

Why Business Plans Fall Flat

Let's be honest: most business plans are full of wishful thinking.

They assume you know what your customers want (you don't, at least not at first). They assume you know something about those customers (you STILL don't, at least not at first!). They also wrongly assume that you know what your margins will be. And they give you a false sense of control.

A strategy accepts reality: that running a small business is messy, unpredictable, and full of trade-offs.

> *"No business plan survives first contact with the customer."*
> *– Steve Blank (American entrepreneur, educator, author and speaker)*

What a Small Business Strategy Actually Looks Like

You don't need a binder. You need clarity on a few key things:

- Who are we for?
- What problem do we solve?
- Why do they pick *us* over someone else?
- How do we make money — and keep making it?
- What are we *not* doing?

Here's a real example:

Jack runs a landscaping company. His strategy? Be the premium provider for two specific, high-income neighbourhoods. He doesn't discount. He doesn't travel outside his zone. His team wears uniforms, his trucks are spotless, and he charges more than his competitors — and still gets more referrals. That's strategy in action.

No spreadsheets. No graphs. Just a series of focused, evidence-based choices that guide the business.

Build Your Small Business Strategy in 4 Simple Steps

You don't need a whiteboard session or a consultant to get started. Just walk through this:

1. Pick a Lane
   Define your ideal customer. Who do you actually want to serve?

2. Clarify Your Edge
   What makes you different or better, and does your customer care?

3. Align Everything Else
   Your pricing, marketing, and operations should support that edge.

4. Say No Often
   Strategy is very much about what you won't do.

You can do this on a napkin — but I'd recommend a one-pager. That's all it takes to anchor your decisions.

Bottom Line: Strategy Beats the Spreadsheet

You don't need a "business plan." You need to know what game you're playing — and how you plan to win it.

Everything else is optional.

Original post URL: https://bradpoulos.com/small-business-strategy/

The $8 Million Problem

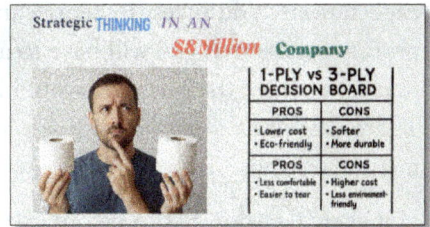

Originally posted on June 28, 2025.

You gotta let go, to Grow.

Back in the 2000s, my brother and I were repping dozens of American suppliers in Canada. After working with so many different owners, we started to notice that they fell into two categories. Some were like us, in that they came from larger organizations and were trying to build a great company, with some structure and ability to scale. But there were more than a few who ran flat organizations and had an intense need to make every single decision. It became a running joke between us that they had an "Eight Million Dollar Problem." Our observation was that anyone can make all the decisions in a company while growing it to $8 million (of course, we meant $USD, and now with inflation, it's 12!). But then, they plateau. Not because of the economy, the product, or the competition, but because the owner has hit capacity.

The Control Trap

These were sharp, hard-working people who had built their businesses from scratch, and along the way they insisted on having the final say on everything from product design, to hiring, to pricing, to purchase orders, to office decor, to choice of cleaning contractors, to bathroom tissue (1 ply vs 2 only. Three? Fuhgeddaboudit!). It wasn't about ego, at least not in an obvious way. From their perspective, it was usually about quality control and making sure things didn't go sideways. But the end result is that the owner became the bottleneck. There are only so many decisions one person can make in a day. So when everything has to go through you, your company can only grow as fast as you can think. That's the ceiling.

What It Takes to Break Through

Getting past that ceiling means moving from owner-led to systems-led. And that means letting go. Not of control, exactly, but of how that control is exercised. Instead of making every decision, you design the systems that guide those decisions. You create clarity around roles, accountability, and expectations. You invest in people and trust them to handle more. Part of the process means that you will have to accept that others will make decisions that differ from the ones you would have made, and that it is perfectly okay. There is always more than one way to do things, and most decisions are not mission-critical.

Not every decision has to be optimized. Sometimes good enough is good enough.

If you're constantly "improving" on the decisions made by those you're supposed to trust, they will not feel the necessary responsibility and autonomy to buy in.

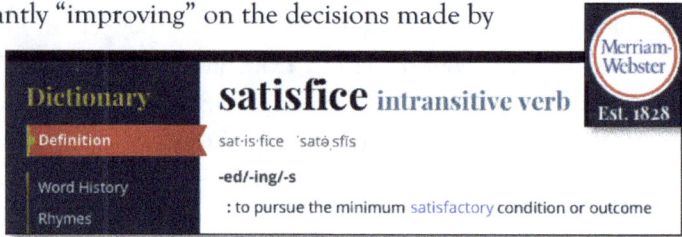

satisfice intransitive verb

sat·is·fice ˈsatəˌsfīs

-ed/-ing/-s

: to pursue the minimum satisfactory condition or outcome

Not every decision has to be fully optimized. Learn to "satisfice".

Why It's So Hard

Letting go is tough because the business is your baby. You've built it with sweat and sacrifice, and no one will ever care about it as much as you do. That's true. But that truth is also a trap. Fear of mistakes, fear of mediocrity, and fear of losing touch are all valid. But they can paralyze you. And the longer you delay, the more you entrench a culture that depends on you for everything. Eventually, you burn out, and the business stagnates. You can't scale a company if you have to personally approve every minor decision. You can either have control, or you can have growth. You can't have both, at least not the same way.

The Systems Mindset

So what does it look like to scale with systems? It means documenting how key processes work, creating SOPs, and clarifying who owns which decisions. It means developing KPIs so you can monitor performance without micromanaging. Here's a real example: instead of reviewing every quote or proposal, you empower your inside sales team to work within a certain minimum and maximum profit level, and only review quotes outside that band or above a certain dollar amount. And over time, you will hopefully want to increase these thresholds, as staff mature, and you get busier working ON your business.

How to Start Letting Go

The shift doesn't happen overnight. Start small. Identify low-risk decisions you can delegate now. Create templates or playbooks to guide your team. Coach your managers, then let them manage. Expect a few stumbles—they're part of the process. Resist the urge to swoop in unless absolutely necessary. And when mistakes happen (because they will), treat them as coaching opportunities, not proof that only you can do the job. You're not aiming for perfection. You're building capacity.

The Real Cost of Staying in Control

Every day you stay too deep in the weeds, your company pays a price. Growth stalls. Good people leave. Opportunities pass by because you didn't get around to them. Eventually, you become exhausted and frustrated, wondering why things aren't moving like they used to. The $8M problem isn't about market size or timing. It's about getting out of the way.

Original post URL: https://bradpoulos.com/8-million-dollar-problem/

Systems Turn Goals From Dreams Into Reality

Originally posted on July 19, 2025.

The Hidden Cost of Flying Blind

I have a friend/client who owns a manufacturing business. By all appearances, this place really did run like a Swiss watch. She had a tight-knit team, a cool product, and a steady stream of clients, largely due to a well-structured online sales funnel process that resulted in high quality, low-cost, leads for her big-ticket products.

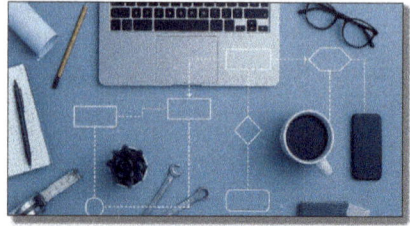

Then one summer, her lead fabricator became ill and was hospitalized right as a huge order came in from a boutique hotel chain. The combination was brutal. Her team scrambled to figure out how he did certain complex builds. Orders backed up. She had to refund two clients and work 14-hour days just to keep the rest from walking.

She didn't realize until then that her business was built on habits, not systems. That summer nearly broke her, not just financially, but mentally, and the sad thing is that it all could have been avoided with a few well-crafted SOPs (Standard Operating Procedures).

This isn't unusual. Many small businesses run on a mix of habits, memory, and verbal instruction. It works, until it doesn't. When the person who "knows how to do it" is out of office or when the business hits a growth curve, chaos sets in.

It's a cousin of another problem I call the 8 Million Dollar problem (see previous post).

The truth is, flying by the seat of your pants doesn't scale. Standard operating procedures (SOPs) aren't bureaucratic busywork. They are the nervous system of a resilient business. And by looking at your business through the lens of systems thinking, the need for SOPs becomes not just obvious, but urgent.

They're an important first step to working on your business rather than in it.

Your Business is More Than the Sum of Its Parts

General Systems Theory came out of biology, thanks to Ludwig von Bertalanffy, who wanted to understand how living organisms maintain stability while interacting with their environments. Over time, this theory was adopted in the world of management, offering a new way to think about organizations.

Instead of viewing a business as a machine made of isolated parts, systems thinking treats it as a dynamic, open, interconnected system that constantly exchanges information, energy, and resources with its environment and itself. Everything from customer feedback to market trends to internal communication loops shapes how the organization functions.

Because of its interdependent nature, a tweak in one area can have a ripple effect across the whole firm. Without that systems awareness, your business decisions may cause more problems than they solve.

Every business creates value by turning inputs into outputs through a transformation process. Whether it's flour into croissants or client briefs into campaigns, this model highlights the importance of understanding, optimizing, and documenting each step so it can be repeated and scaled effectively.

And we don't stop at the point of delivery. What happens afterward is just as important. Customer complaints, repeat orders, online reviews, and even support tickets all form part of a feedback loop that informs how well your overall system is working. If you're not capturing and using this information, you're flying blind. Feedback loops allow your business to self-correct and improve over time; they're a core feature of any well-designed system.

Understanding where your business ends (and thus, where your systems' boundaries lie). These are the factors you control.

But no business operates in isolation. You're always part of a larger ecosystem. Things like competitors, regulations, supply chain disruptions, and customer preferences lie outside, but still affect your system significantly. Knowing what you control, and what you must respond to, helps you focus your energy on the right priorities, without wasting time on things you can't control.

Taking that to the extreme however results in rigid thinking. One of the core concepts of a systems approach is the notion of equifinality. There isn't just one path to success. Two businesses can take very different approaches and still arrive at equally strong outcomes. What matters is whether the system as a whole can adapt, learn, and deliver on its goals.

Your Business's Operating System

SOPs are more than just checklists. They are the architecture behind how your business actually works. When approached through a systems lens, they become tools for designing consistency, clarity, and adaptability into your operations.

This means creating SOPs that account for the full customer journey, not just internal tasks. It means capturing the way your team thinks and makes decisions. It means designing feedback into the process so things improve over time. And it means aligning your SOPs with your goals and incentives— so you're not just documenting what people do, but shaping what they strive to do better.

Good SOPs make people smarter, not replace them. They reduce cognitive load, preserve institutional memory, and build in guardrails that reduce errors. In systems terms, SOPs are both knowledge hubs and safety nets.

Systems Thinking – A Small Business Systems Advantage

Small businesses don't have the luxury of excess. Every mistake hits harder when resources are tight. And when critical knowledge lives in just one person's head, the whole operation becomes fragile. SOPs reduce this risk by capturing that knowledge and turning it into something repeatable.

They also prepare a business for growth. As complexity increases, documented systems prevent things from falling through the cracks. And perhaps most importantly, good SOPs allow you to respond to market changes quickly.

Systems thinking gives small businesses an edge by enabling them to learn and adapt faster than competitors. SOPs play a critical role here. They support personal mastery by helping individuals refine and repeat best practices. They enable team learning by making processes visible, consistent, and improvable. And they anchor a shared vision by embedding company values and direction into the way work gets done every day.

Building Your Systems-Based SOP Framework

Before you document anything, you need a clear view of what matters most. That's where a systems audit comes in. Start by identifying the critical paths in your business. What are the essential workflows that keep things moving? Then, map how information flows (or fails to flow) throughout the business. Finally, define your boundaries: What falls within your control and needs documenting, and what lives outside your system?

Once you've mapped the system, treat your SOPs like living documents. That means version control so your team always uses the latest version. It means baking in feedback loops so your systems evolve as your business does. And it means making SOPs part of the culture, something people use and can personally see value in, not just file away.

As your SOPs mature, they can evolve beyond static instructions into dynamic tools for resilience and innovation. Good systems help your business bounce back from setbacks by reducing chaos and clarifying decision-making. They allow for exceptions, making room for judgment without breaking structure. And when the basics are in place, real creativity can emerge.

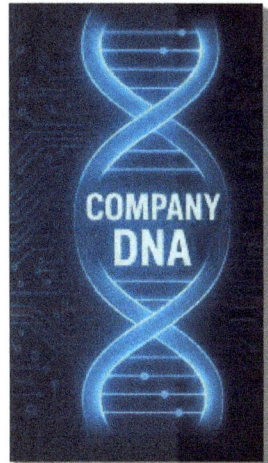

SOPs also link different parts of your business together. They coordinate cross-functional workflows, integrate smoothly with suppliers and customers, and amplify the value of your digital tools. In short, they connect the dots—internally and externally—so the whole business runs more smoothly.

Implementation Roadmap: From Chaos to System

Like so many other things, getting started is often the most difficult part. A simple 90-day roadmap can make all the difference: spend the first two weeks identifying priorities and doing a systems audit. Use the next six weeks to document your core processes. Then use the final month to test, refine, and train your team.

Track your progress using a mix of early signals and long-term results. Look at things like process consistency, training time, and error rates. Over time, monitor broader metrics like customer satisfaction, employee retention, and growth. Most importantly, make sure your SOPs include a built-in loop for ongoing improvement.

Your Business as an Intelligent System

When you build good systems, the payoff is real. In the short term, you get more consistency and fewer mistakes. Over time, those small improvements compound into a smarter, more resilient organization. And paradoxically, the more structure you have, the more freedom you gain to focus, to delegate, and to grow.

If you're not sure where to start, pick one process that breaks often or frustrates your team. Turn that into your first SOP. Once you see the benefits, momentum builds. While your competitors keep winging it, you'll have a system that gets better every day.

Further Reading

If you'd like to go deeper into the theory behind this subject check out the following:

Kast, F. E., & Rosenzweig, J. E. (1972).
General systems theory: Applications for organization and management.
Academy of Management Journal.

Monat, J., Amissah, M., & Gannon, T. (2020).
Practical applications of systems thinking to business.

Hudson, M., Smart, A., & Bourne, M. (2001).
Theory and practice in SME performance measurement systems.
International Journal of Operations & Production Management.

Original post URL: https://bradpoulos.com/systems-thinking/

Why The Owner Must Review Every Hire

Originally posted on July 15, 2025.

New Hires: The Most Important Decisions You'll Make.

Every small business owner has a story about the one hire they wish they could do over. Turns out the person had the skills, but not the values. Sure, they looked good on paper, but they were a poor fit for the culture. In small teams, there's no place to hide that.

It's been my experience that when we've made a bad hire, it wasn't the person's ability to do the job or their technical skills, that were the misfit. Our managers were good at discriminating between those who could do the job and those who couldn't. Hiring mistakes almost always came down to a bad cultural fit.

The stakes are high. In a 1,000-person firm, a bad hire might go unnoticed for months and never create a blip on the income statement. In a 10-person team, everyone feels it by Friday. One values mismatch can breed tension, erode trust, and slow everything down. It's disruptive, and it's a missed chance to bring in someone who could have moved the culture forward.

The costs involved in rectifying such a mistake can be as high as 50% of the position's salary, and this may not fully account for indirect or opportunity costs, including lost productivity, damage to morale, or potential harm to customer relationships. In a big company, the CEO can downsource the culture job to direct reports or even part of the HR department, but in a small business, it's on the owner. When it's well done, everyone adopts it as part of their role, but the ultimate responsibility lies with the owner.

That means that the small business owner must personally review every hire; not to second-guess skills, but to protect and shape the firm's culture.

Culture Is the Ultimate Competitive Advantage

I've written previously about the importance of culture in a small business. Think of culture as how people behave when no one is watching. It's a mix of unwritten rules, shared values, and everyday behaviours that guide decisions and shape how work gets done. It shows up in how your team handles customer complaints, shares credit, communicates across departments, and even how they show up on Monday morning.

Get it right, and you have a team that runs smoothly, treats customers well, and sticks around. Get it wrong, and you spend your time cleaning up messes. Culture affects everything: customer experience, collaboration, productivity, morale, and brand reputation.

And here's the thing: culture isn't what you say. Culture is what you tolerate, reward, and do. You can have all the values posters in the world, but they mean nothing if behaviour and decisions don't align.

Great companies like Trader Joe's, Shopify, and Firespring are recognized for their distinctive cultures. That didn't happen by accident. It happened because someone at the top made culture their job.

Hiring for Values

I can say with complete confidence that no one was ever hired in a company I owned or ran that I didn't personally interview. My role was to be the final cultural gatekeeper. I had a veto. This was to ensure that they were not just a technical fit, which would have been predetermined by their potential manager, but also a cultural fit.

Not once did I ever use my veto. I suppose that's a testament to how well our management embodied our values every day.

Your hiring process should also aim to do that. Early in the process, you should transcend any technical examination and assess the candidate on their character, integrity, and motivation.

Look at how they treated the receptionist. Did they display a collaborative or autonomous decision-making style? Did they ask thoughtful questions or just sell themselves? Did they display some humility to go along with their ego?

Ask Value-Centric Questions

Try asking some value-testing questions like:

- "Tell me about a time you made a decision that wasn't popular but felt right to you."
- "How do you handle situations where your manager is wrong?"
- "What kind of work environment brings out your best?"

Listen for their personal values, not polished answers. Try to uncover a bit of their personality and character.

Topping the process off with a final interview with the owner sends a clear message: culture matters here. It keeps change intentional and evolutionary, and gives the owner a chance to gently steer the culture in a deliberate direction.

"But I Don't Have Time to Interview Everyone"

You might think you don't have time to interview every hire. But the truth is, you don't have time not to. A single bad hire, especially in a customer-facing or leadership role, can cost thousands in lost productivity, morale, and customer trust.

The cultural fit conversation doesn't need to take an hour. Even 15 minutes of focused questions can reveal a lot. Let others handle the technical screening, but never outsource the final call. That's your job.

Bring Your Personality To The Process

From 1999 to 2006, Jeff Bezos famously made a point of asking every Amazon candidate a deceptively simple question about mindset:
"On a scale from 1 to 10, how much do you attribute your success to luck?"

The goal wasn't humility or ego; it was insight into mindset. Those who recognize a blend of personal effort and external opportunity tend to stay grounded, motivated, and resilient, all key traits for thriving in high-pressure, innovative environments like Amazon.

For years, I asked every final-round candidate one of a handful of questions. Never about their resume, but about who they were.

One I borrowed from my brother applied only to sales people. I would casually ask them what salary that they had asked for (as if I didn't already know!), and then regardless of what their number was I would look at them stone-faced and ask, "what on earth makes you think you're worth that kind of money?"

I was intentionally being a bit confrontational to see how they'd react when a customer challenged them. It's particularly powerful when they're asking for a reasonable salary, but better to find out now that you're hiring a salesperson who doesn't like to be challenged.

Another favourite was to ask them what their last (or current) manager would say about them.

The Owner is the Culture Architect

Culture is built one hire at a time. It doesn't take many people to change the tone of a small company, for better or worse. That's why the owner must stay close to hiring. You set the tone. You decide who gets in. And that final interview? It's your last line of defense.

Original post URL: https://bradpoulos.com/hiring-for-culture/

The Surprising Power of Strategic Inaction

Originally posted on July 29, 2025.

Doing nothing may be the best move you can make

Most Problems Solve Themselves

It might sound lazy, but it's based on experience. I first discovered this during the busiest period of my career. I was a Sales Manager who was also running an internal startup called DirecPC (Canada's first satellite-based internet access solution), all while doing a part-time MBA, and trying to be some kind of dad to my two preschool kids.

I was so busy that I just naturally defaulted to waiting until people asked for things a second and third time before responding or complying.

It revealed what became my second law of management:

> *Left alone, 90% of problems solve themselves.*
> *- Brad Poulos*

You see, a lot of those "problems" never warranted follow-up by the initiator. I just never heard about it again. There *was* no second email, *and* no disasters occurred. I don't remember anything ever blowing up in my face because of my "inattention" to detail. It was incredibly eye-opening. I slowly adopted the attitude that, "Well, if you're not willing to at least ask twice..."

Ever since, I've applied this principle—be selective about what problems you jump on—throughout my business and personal lives.

Strategic Inaction

Many so-called 'problems' are actually quite fleeting. Priorities shift, rendering an issue inconsequential. Often, a simple misunderstanding or miscommunication can cause brief consternation. By letting the dust settle instead of immediately intervening, you give the situation time to breathe, messages to percolate, discussions to unfold, and the truth to emerge.

Jumping in too quickly can actually make matters worse, turning minor hiccups into real issues. In many cases, if left alone, teams and systems will correct themselves. The challenge is that leaders often feel compelled to control everything, when in fact, stepping back can be the smarter, more effective move.

I Didn't Invent This: Modern Application of a Timeless Idea

This principle isn't entirely new. In fact, it echoes ideas found in several domains.

In Eastern philosophy, both Buddhism and Daoism teach the value of calm observation and non-reactivity.

The Daoist concept of wu wei (non-doing or effortless action) perfectly captures the spirit of strategic inaction.

Systems Thinking in the Wild

Systems thinking also supports this view. In complex environments, problems often contain the seeds of their own resolution. Feedback loops emerge, behaviour self-corrects, and balance is restored without top-down interference.

Think about how a population of rabbits in a forest might cause overgrazing if it increases too rapidly, but then attract more foxes, hawks and other predators that consume them, reducing the population of rabbits, and with them, predators, due to a decline in their available food source. Ecosystem balance is maintained by two negative feedback loops that continually interact without any external management. Or how, when a road becomes congested, drivers may seek alternative routes and adjust travel times, redistributing traffic more evenly, reducing congestion on the original road, and restoring balance.

Decision Theory and Behavioural Insight

Decision theory adds another layer; waiting can be a powerful strategy.

Postponing a decision doesn't always reflect indecisiveness; it can allow for clarity, perspective, or the resolution of the issue altogether.

Lastly, behavioural science reveals that humans are prone to cognitive biases. We often overestimate the urgency or magnitude of problems in the heat of the moment. Time brings context, and with it, the realization that many issues were never as important as they first appeared.

When It Doesn't Work

Of course, not every problem should be ignored. The skilled small business manager can identify the critical 10% that do require swift and decisive action. Those issues that carry serious consequences (threats to safety, legal liability, deep structural failures, reputational risks) demand immediate attention, not strategic inaction.

But the remaining 90%?

Let Them Marinate

Doing nothing is not the same as being passive or negligent. It's an active choice rooted in experience and judgment. It is about selective action, not avoidance. When used wisely, it's a powerful management tool.

Some big issue gnawing at you?

Maybe you should let the universe handle it. You've got enough on your plate!

Original post URL: https://bradpoulos.com/strategic-inaction/

The Small Business Health Check

Originally posted on August 9, 2025.

Quarterly Tasks Every Owner Should Have on Autopilot

Running a small business means living in the trenches. Folks like me love to espouse the need to work "on your businesses" while you're juggling sales, operations, marketing, people, and cash, plus whatever issues you have at home! Much easier said than done.

But what separates effective small business owners from reactive ones is a disciplined quarterly rhythm. Consistency is key. Here are the ten tasks every small business owner should put on autopilot every 90 days. If you have a bookkeeper, this should be their job. If you're still doing this yourself, get yourself a bookkeeper!

1. Check Your Cash

Start with the basics. How much money is in the bank? Do you know how much is coming in next month? What's going out? If not, now's the time to start tracking this. There's a simple tool on my website[4] that will get you started.

This is one of your most important functions as an owner. You have to know if you can cover payroll, taxes, and suppliers in the near future.

2. Review Sales & Pipeline

How much did you sell this quarter? What's in the pipeline? Are leads moving forward or sitting idle? If you're a typical industrial or B-to-B business, you should be tracking three things:

- New booked business – how much new business did you sell, or "book", this period? This is a measure of the sales team's effectiveness.

---

[4] *https://bradpoulos.com/business-resources/#CashFlowPlanning*

- Orders Shipped – how much product or service was delivered and invoiced during the period. This is a measure of the operation's effectiveness.

- Current backlog – how much business do you have "in the bag" in the sense that you've made the sale (booked it), but haven't yet shipped it or counted the revenues. This is a typical goldilocks situation. If it gets too low, you could have an operation that's twiddling their thumbs soon. If it gets too high, you might be taking too long to deliver and making customers unhappy. The art is always in the interpretation, not the generation, of the numbers.

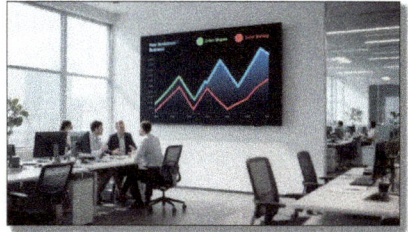

These three key indicators should be tracked constantly, and reported to the entire operation, ideally visually, using a graph.

If you're a retail business, how are sales tracking vs last year at this time? Do you know your sales per square foot, average basket size (also called average transaction value), and inventory turnover?

3. Inspect Key Metrics and Profitability

Track a handful of KPIs that matter to your business. Don't drown in data. Combine leading (activity) and lagging(results) indicators, and include basic financial performance like gross margin and net profit. Like so many things, this will be somewhat unique to your business:

- A local coffee shop might track: daily foot traffic, average spend per customer, and food cost as a percentage of revenue.
- A retail clothing store could monitor: sales per square foot, inventory turnover rate, and return percentage.
- A real estate agent might track open house traffic or website visits.
- A SaaS business might look at: churn rate, monthly recurring revenue (MRR), and customer acquisition cost (CAC).
- A small manufacturing firm might track: machine utilization rates, units produced per labour hour, and on-time delivery rate.
- A professional services business could measure: billable hours per

consultant, average project margin, and client satisfaction scores.

- A cleaning company might monitor: average tenure of clients, average revenue per job, and % of cleaning jobs with complaints.

The trick is to choose the right metrics for your business. There's no one right set of measures. You need to identify the key success factors of your industry, and measure those.

PRO TIP: Create dashboards for daily or weekly tracking.

What's Your "One Big Number"

For slightly larger businesses, I suggest the owner identify their "one big number". I don't mean big as in large, but rather in importance. Every CEO has a pile of things that they have to keep on their radar, but it helps if they can reduce their entire operation to "ONE BIG NUMBER" that identifies that one most important thing. You can't use the bottom line because that applies to everyone. It has to be an operational or financial measure, ideally a leading indicator, since that allows for earlier intervention when needed.

For businesses with a long sales cycle it might be win rate or sales velocity. Any high-growth company will be looking at revenue or subscriber (or some other) growth metric. A clothing retailer might look at GMROI (Gross Margin Return on Investment (it's just what it sounds like!).

One interesting example from my past is the perspective of the CEO of a cannabis grower. Since the industry, sadly, seems to focus on THC potency above all else, I posit that such CEO should care most about their cost to produce a milligram of THC.

---

4. Review Human Resources & Training

Even with a small team, take a step back to assess performance, development needs, and hiring plans. Are you set up to support growth? Who needs support or recognition? Who is vital to the team and would leave you in a tough position if they left? Deal with these issues now.

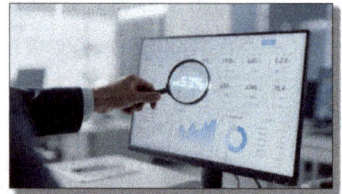

5. Check In With Customers

It doesn't matter if your business serves hundreds or thousands of retail customers or only a handful of high-value, high-touch clients. The questions are still the same:

- Do they believe that you deliver good value?
- Do or would they recommend you to others?
- Do they intend to continue doing business with you?

The specific questions and how you get the answers will be unique to your business. It might be very unscientific, unstructured, and highly personal or you might use tools like feedback surveys, online reviews and NPS scores to identify trends and opportunities.

6. Review Marketing, Website & SEO

Your quarterly review should look at whether you're achieving the goals of your marketing plan. You have one, right?! If you had plans for advertising, or content creation, or any other marketing activity that didn't happen, analyze why.

In many small businesses, marketing is an add-on function to an individual's main job, and can suffer as a result. Whatever the reason, identify why and resolve the bottleneck.

7. Assess IT, Security & Digital Tools

The cloud has made many business functions a lot easier. You might think that this means that you needn't worry about backing up key data. While cloud services typically have their own backups, it's essential to understand the shared responsibility you may have. In 2019 Salesforce customers lost data after a major outage. And many custom applications are still hosted on site, where you'll need to ensure that off-site backups are being created. Do you have the necessary cybersecurity and access controls. Are passwords changed regularly? Almost none of us do. This is a good time to audit what you have and cancel unused software.

8. Inventory Management (if applicable)

You don't all carry inventory, and those that do will have different approaches. This is the time to review turnover, shrinkage, and stockout frequency, and adjust reorder points to optimize slow-moving SKUs. You might ask if there is any part of your business that can take advantage of drop shipping (items are shipped directly from the supplier to the customer), allowing you to eliminate some inventory cost.

9. Premises Audit

What is the state of your physical operations? Do the inside and outside of your premises look clean and tidy? Do they make you proud and reflect your values? Appearances matter. A professional-looking environment will breed professionalism just as having crap all over the floors everywhere sends the message that the little things are not important.

- Do the walls need painting or carpets need cleaning or replacing?
- Do you have appropriate and sufficient signage?
- Are the appropriate safety measures in place?
- Do you have or should you create a maintenance schedule?

10. Review SOPs, Innovation & Growth Readiness

Are your systems ready to support more growth? What's outdated? What's undocumented? Use this checkpoint to sharpen your processes. Choose one area to document or refine in the next quarter. Here's some help.

Systematize It or It Won't Stick

If it's not on your calendar, it doesn't exist. Make these quarterly reviews recurring events. Delegate where possible. Build a dashboard (even a simple spreadsheet) that brings everything together. And keep it lean. If your quarterly review takes more than half a day, you're overcomplicating it. This isn't busywork. It's the difference between running your business and being run by it.

Original post URL: https://bradpoulos.com/small-business-health-check

Customer Warning Signs: How to Spot Trouble Before It Hits Your Business

Originally posted on August 12, 2025.

In 2005, Nortel was still Canada's largest company, but the slide had already begun. They were our biggest customer, and represented about 30% of our business. One day, they just announced that payment terms would change from 45 to 60 days, and that acceptance of future purchase orders was tacit acceptance of these terms.

It was the second red flag in as many quarters. The first had been the shift of accounts payable to a third-party outfit in Nashville. I used to refer to them as the payment prevention department. Overnight, payment questions fell into a black hole. It became impossible to reach anyone inside Nortel who could deal with any kind of payment problem.

The 15-day extension was the tipping point. I gathered our inside sales team and told them to apply "special" pricing on all Nortel quotes going forward. Take whatever we would charge any other customer for something, and add 5%.

The sales team looked at me bewildered. I told them I was serious. Call it a "Nortel tax." And to let me know if there was any pushback.

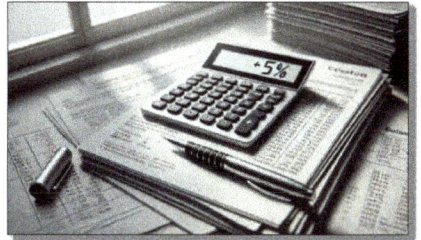

My thinking about this was the same as for a prepayment discount. I was effectively giving them a 15-day loan in the form of extra time to pay, and I was "charging" them 5% for that loan. That's 5% divided by 15 days, or 0.33% per day, which is 122% return per annum on my "investment" in the extra accounts receivable (actually, it's 333% if you compound it! $1.0033^{365} = 3.33$).

Surprise, surprise! They never pushed back. Not once. That told me two things:

- they weren't watching costs closely. Their eye was off the ball; and
- they were bleeding cash, so they cared more about how long they had to pay than the amount they had to pay.

As my dad would say, they had the em-*PHA*-sis on the wrong syl-*LA*-ble.

Nortel filed for bankruptcy in 2009. The decline was visible years earlier to anyone watching the right signals.

Customer Warning Signs Matter

When a big client's finances get shaky, suppliers as unsecured creditors are usually the first to feel the pain when the collapse comes. Large accounts can lull you into a false sense of security because they keep placing orders, even as their fundamentals weaken, and they slowly stretch payment terms, growing their debt.

The risk is even greater if one customer represents a large share of your revenue. That's concentration risk, and it's dangerous. One bankruptcy can take you down with them.

During the heyday of the dot-com boom, we had a customer, Maxlink, that was building a wireless network across Canada for commercial data service. Thankfully, and due to no good management and purely good luck, the day they went bankrupt, they owed us nothing. But just one month prior, they owed us over $1 million. That amount of bad debt would have spelled bankruptcy for our small company, which had only $11.5 million in sales that year.

We had let the allure of large orders from (supposedly) large customers overtake our judgment.

When the Giants Stumble

There are two simple takeaways here.

The first warning is not to let a big customer's volume seduce you into financing their problems. When a client starts paying with time instead of cash—moving A/P offsite, extending terms unilaterally, and shrugging at price increases—it's a flashing red light that your risk is increasing.

The second is that just because they're big doesn't mean they're good. Sometimes they're so big they don't notice or don't care about modest changes. We bumped their costs by 5% and they didn't blink!

If the biggest company in the country can go bankrupt, anyone can. Your job, as always, is to have your eye on your business, read the signals early, treat credit like the loan it is, and make sure no single account can take you down with them.

Original post URL: https://bradpoulos.com/customer-warning-signs/

Before You Scale, Do the Math

Originally posted on August 30, 2025.

The Case for Unit Economics

When I was a kid, one of the big muffler companies ran TV ads where the final line, delivered by the journeyman muffler fixer guy to his understudy, was, "first you get good, then you get fast."

For some reason, this has always stuck with me, such that over the years I've adopted and modified the saying as a metaphor for many business concepts, most often when a startup should turn on the jets and start to scale:

> *First you get good, then you get big!"*
> *– Brad Poulos*

Developing an intimate understanding of your unit economics is one of the smartest things you can do in the early days of your business. Before you start scaling, spending heavily on marketing, or chasing investors, you need to know whether your core offer makes money. And not just overall. You need to know if it makes money one unit at a time.

Unit economics is about simplicity. It's the revenue and cost associated with a single "unit" of your product or service. That might be one physical widget, one burger, one hour of service, one customer, or one subscription. It's your business in miniature. And if the math doesn't work at the unit level, it certainly won't work when you grow.

What Are Unit Economics, Really?

The "unit" depends on your business model, but the core principles are the same. Unit economics focuses on what happens each time you sell one more unit. At a basic level, you're tracking:

- Revenue per unit: What you earn every time you deliver one unit.
- Variable cost per unit: What it costs to make and deliver that unit.
- Contribution margin: The amount left over after subtracting variable costs from revenue. This is what contributes to covering your fixed costs and, eventually, generating profit.

Fixed costs such as rent or salaries are not a factor until later when we look a breakeven point.

Why You Need to Nail This Early

Too many early-stage entrepreneurs skip this step. They assume that growth will solve their problems. But if you haven't nailed your unit economics, growth can just multiply losses. Even more insidious is when it's clear that there's some positive contribution margin, but you find out that it's so low that i you'll have to sell 49 bajillion whatevers to cover fixed costs.

When you understand your cost structure early on, you:

- Price your offer with confidence (and not guesswork).
- Choose better marketing and sales channels.
- Spot red flags before they turn into disasters.
- Show credibility to investors and lenders.

It's not about having perfect data from day one. It's about having directionally correct numbers that help you make better decisions.

A Simple Example

Let's say you sell a product for $100. Your cost to produce and ship it is $40. That means your contribution margin is $60. That $60 goes toward covering your rent, paying your team, promoting the product, and eventually, building profit.

Now imagine you reduce your cost by $5 or raise your price by $5. That's an extra $5 of margin per unit. Sell 1,000 units and you've found $5,000 in extra profitability.

The same applies for services. If you charge $150/hour and pay your subcontractor $90/hour, you've got $60/hour in contribution margin. If that doesn't feel like enough to cover your overhead, you've got a pricing or efficiency problem.

Don't confuse contribution margin with gross profit. The latter includes only Cost of Goods Sold (COGS) which are often called "direct" costs. It doesn't include all of the company's "variable" costs which are things that will increase with sales volume, but fall into fixed costs if you listen to the accountants. This would include such things as customer support, returns, and customer onboarding.

Solid Unit Economics Looks Like...

Shoot for at least three out of the following:

- A strongly positive contribution margin.
- A realistic breakeven point (a reasonable sales level will cover fixed costs).
- Some degree of scalability (costs don't rise 1:1 with revenue).
- An ability to profitably acquire a customer over time.

If your numbers don't reflect this yet, that's okay. It's better to know now than later, before you waste valuable resources trying to scale an inefficient operation. Work on lowering costs or increasing customer value so you can raise your price until you have something worth scaling.

Be careful and avoid these common mistakes.

- Including only Cost of Goods Sold as opposed to all of the variable costs;
- Forgetting to factor in discounts, freebies, and other revenue-reducers; and
- Assuming growth automatically brings profitability.

Tune the Engine Before You Hit the Gas

Scaling a company without understanding your unit economics is like trying to build speed in a car without checking if the engine actually works. You might make noise, burn fuel, and even move forward, but you're more likely to sputter across the line than win the race.

That's why "first you get good, then you get big" isn't just a clever saying, it's a survival strategy. Good means profitable, at the unit level. Big only makes sense when the math works.

So before you step on the gas, pop the hood. Run the numbers. Tune the engine. Then, when it's time to scale, you'll know you're driving something that can actually win.

Original post URL: https://bradpoulos.com/unit-economics

AI for Small Business: Practical Tools and Use Cases

Originally posted on September 2, 2025.

Free up hours, cut costs, and boost consistency.

AI isn't the future for small businesses. It's now.

Thanks mostly to the launch of ChatGPT three years ago, the term AI is everywhere. AI isn't new, but the proliferation of new capabilities is. The past few years have seen a gush of new generative Artificial Intelligence (AI) applications that can fundamentally transform how some of our work gets done. Generative AI is a type of artificial intelligence that creates new content, including text, images, audio, video, or even computer programming code, based on patterns it has learned from vast amounts of existing data. Instead of simply retrieving or classifying information, it uses machine learning models, most often large language models (LLMs) or diffusion models, to predict what comes next in a sequence.

This allows it to "generate" outputs that can be original in form while still reflecting the style, structure, and context of its training data and the input prompt. Common examples include chatbots that write articles or answer questions, image generators that produce realistic or artistic visuals from a text prompt, and tools that compose music or design prototypes.

There are thousands of gen AI tools available now, and names such as ChatGPT, Gemini, CoPilot, Perplexity, and Claude are entering the vernacular. Normally offered as a web app, making them accessible and ubiquitous, these tools are helping shave hours off administrative tasks, improve response times, and make marketing materials more consistently reflect a coherent brand voice.

While generative AI can dramatically speed up creative and analytical tasks, it is still in its infancy, and sometimes says things that reveal its tender age. Its results still require human review for accuracy, ethics, and alignment with intended goals.

In short, AI can be wrong and sometimes hallucinates! Use it blindly at your peril!

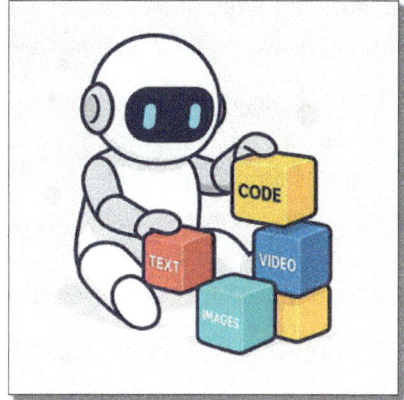

Not all AI is Generative AI

We won't dwell on it here because for now, gen AI is where it's at for small business owners, but there are many other types of AI that don't create new content. It's all over the place. AI engines recommend your next online purchase or Netflix movie. Predictive analytics helps foresee and avoid equipment failures. Classification models are used by your email provider to sort emails into "spam" or "not spam," and flag fraudulent transactions to your credit card companies. Delivery and logistics companies use optimization algorithms to route trucks for the shortest travel time or most energy efficiency.

In the future, AI tools will help physicians and other clinicians diagnose and even predict disease or disorders in patients. Signals will be controlled in real time so route traffic can be optimally routed in areas where congestion is a problem. The number of potential use cases is unlimited and while some small businesses should pursue these sorts of AI tools in their operations, we will concern ourselves here with generative AI.

What Generative AI Actually Does (Plain English)

Think of it as pattern recognition, plus autocomplete.

It studies piles of examples, spots patterns, and predicts what likely comes next. From that, it can summarize long content into key points, draft emails and posts, classify and tag information, recommend next steps, and surface similar items. Hooked up to your apps, it can fetch facts, create tasks, fill forms, and nudge you with reminders so routine work moves faster and stays organized. Myriad forms of output are possible including text, images, ppt files, spreadsheets, computer code and audio/video.

It's best at clear, well-structured tasks where examples exist. Give it context, a goal, and a tone, and it will produce a first pass you can refine. It handles variations quickly (multiple subject lines, product blurbs, or code snippets) and it keeps format and style consistent. It's also useful for extracting data from text, summarizing meetings, and proposing next-best actions based on past patterns. With basic tool access, it can update a calendar invite, draft a follow-up, or log notes in your system.

In most cases today it remains an assistant, not a replacement. You set intent, provide constraints, and make the call; it does the groundwork and iterations. Treat it like a hyper-capable junior: very fast, with an abundance of energy, and occasionally wrong. Very wrong. These are the jobs that will be replaced by AI. Junior positions.

Here are some real use cases of my own that will help to drive this home.

Early Startup Research

Earlier this year, I visited Della Terra in St. Catharines, ON, a specialty shop that sells mostly olive oils and balsamic vinegars. It's a beautiful little store with very good quality products and a terrific vibe. The concept was new to me and I was intrigued by it, so when I got home I put this prompt into ChatGPT:

> *Have a look around Southern Ontario at every town larger than 25,000 people and see whether or not they have an olive oil shop. Tell me which ones do and which ones don't. Give me a summary of the current operators in the province regardless of community size.*

Below is a screenshot of the first bit of the response, which took 2 minutes and 9 seconds and an unimaginable amount of computing power to provide.

Thought for 2m 9s >

Got it. "Olive-oil shop" here = a dedicated retail/tasting room focused on extra-virgin olive oils and balsamic vinegars (not just a grocery/stockist). I did a first pass across Southern Ontario's 25k+ towns and flagged places where I could **not** find a dedicated shop *within the municipal limits* (nearby towns may have one).

There's a lot going on here. The model was smart enough to add the criteria to rule out stockists or those who merely carry the products of others along with a large variety of other products, thus not qualifying as a specialty olive oil shop.

A few prompts later and I had a detailed listing of all the competition in the province, and the locations that looked promising for a new operation.

I knew their address, website, and basic offerings.

map showing AI being used for small business research

This all took less than 10 minutes. Three years ago, it would have taken a junior marketing person at least two days to get this information back to me.

Summarizing Feedback

Each year, I conduct an end-of-year exercise with our graduating entrepreneurship students, in which they provide recommendations on what activities we should Stop, Start, and Continue. We use a word cloud tool (Menti) that allows students to submit words or phrases, which are then displayed and updated on the screen in real time.

I then pick and choose themes from the word cloud for discussion during the class.

Although the submissions can be exported to a spreadsheet, the class size of 100 students leads to significant duplication, with numerous recurring themes across three documents (Stop, Start, Continue), each containing approximately 100 responses. Additionally, there is overlap between the documents, as certain issues may be positioned as either a start or stop.

The last time we did this I submitted the three excel docs to ChatGPT and asked it to analyze and summarize them, eliminating duplicates and grouping the comments into common themes. The setup took 1 minute, the response took 1 second, and this all saved me at least an hour.

But this is what I call "monkey work". It doesn't take smarts. It just takes time (for humans, that is). So "monkey workers" should probably be worried about their jobs.

Helping with "Blank Page Syndrome"

Blank page syndrome is real. That sinking feeling when you're supposed to create something smart and useful, but all you've got is an empty screen. It happens to everyone—even experienced writers.

This is where generative AI shines. Instead of sitting stuck, you can toss it a handful of keywords, a rough outline, or even just an idea that isn't fully formed yet. In seconds, you've got a draft to react to.

Whether you're drafting a business proposal, newsletter, or report, AI helps you get moving and lowers the barrier to creativity.

I hope you're not surprised that I leaned on ChatGPT and Perplexity in writing and researching this very piece.

Marketing & Content, Quicker Campaigns, Consistent Output

Marketing is a great place to start looking for opportunities to leverage AI tools. Here's how you might use AI to draft your next newsletter and create three social media posts from it in under 30 minutes. Imagine you have the following objectives:

- Generate newsletter outlines, subject lines, and calls to action tailored to your audience.
- Turn one long post or video into platform-ready snippets and captions.
- Research and identify SEO keyword clusters, draft articles, and produce meta titles/descriptions.
- Brainstorm ad angles, headlines, and copy, then analyze performance summaries.
- Create simple visuals, thumbnails, lightweight graphics, using AI design tools.

Here's a potential prompt for an email campaign:

You are a small-business email marketer. Draft a 200-word newsletter for [audience], promoting [offer] with a friendly, helpful tone. Provide 5 subject lines (max 45 characters) and 3 preview lines. Include one clear CTA.

Similarly here's a potential prompt you could use for drafting a SEO blog:

Create a detailed outline for a 1,000-word blog post about [topic] aimed at [audience]. Include H2/H3s, keyword clusters, 6 FAQs, and suggested internal links based on [list your pages].

HR Policies

You aren't big enough to have a dedicated HR person. Unfortunately, that's you! But you've come to the point that you think you should have some policies around hours, pay, leave, etc. so that you and your management make decisions fairly and consistently.

You have Google Gemini create the first draft with this prompt:

You are an HR consultant for a 15-person small business. Create a clear, simple set of HR policies covering hours of work, overtime, vacation/leave, pay periods, statutory

> holidays, sick leave, workplace conduct and ANY OTHER
> AREAS YOU THINK ARE APPROPRIATE. The policies
> should be written in plain language (9th grade reading level),
> no legal jargon, and formatted as a handbook-style document
> with headings and bullet points. Include a short introduction
> about why policies matter for fairness and consistency. Flag
> any areas that may require review with a local employment
> lawyer or government labor standards. Keep the draft concise.

Gen AI is still a Baby

I laugh when I hear about how AI is going to replace all of our jobs.

It's almost a ritual: each new wave of technology arrives, surrounded by anxious predictions that it will render us all obsolete. Do you know what else was supposed to replace us?

- The cotton gin
- The computer
- The personal computer
- The internet
- Robots

Each of these, at the margin, did indeed eliminate jobs some jobs, at the margin. But taken as a whole they are multiplicative. They make a society more productive. Think about where we'd be without the internet. It's almost unthinkable. The benefits it has brought to society are immeasurable, but not without casualties.

How would you like to be a travel agent right now?

Or a magazine publisher?

Record store?

Phone directory ad salesperson?

AI won't be any different. There will be a combination of winners and losers, with most of us being winners, one hopes.

Don't lose sight of the fact that AI is still a baby. These tools will literally make up facts. Like any tool, used without care, it can be dangerous. A combination of AI with a lack of critical thinking could lead to embarrassing and costly mistakes. Check everything!

Also, be careful about pasting sensitive info into unvetted tools. User agreements universally favour those writing them, and as a general rule, I would avoid use of any personal data with these tools.

Not sure where to start? Ask ChatGPT (Or Perplexity, or Gemini, or Copilot, or Genspark)

Let's get real meta and ask AI how you should use AI in your small business. Use something like the following prompt in any of the popular LLMs and see what comes out:

"I am the owner of a small business in the [industry] sector, located in [country/region]. My business has about [number] employees and our main challenges are [list top 2–3 pain points, e.g., marketing consistency, customer service load, inventory management]. Act as a consultant who specializes in applying AI for small businesses. Suggest practical, low-cost ways I can use AI tools to improve efficiency, save time, or increase revenue in my business. Please give me ideas across different areas such as marketing, sales, operations, finance, and HR. For each idea, explain the benefit, suggest the type of AI tool to use, and give one simple example prompt I could try."

Every successful small business owner that I know is a lifelong learner. AI is just another opportunity for you to set yourself apart and use your critical faculties to find ways to leverage these powerful tools, while avoiding the rabbit holes that many go down.

Start small. Measure everything. Keep what works.

Original post URL: https://bradpoulos.com/ai-for-small-business/

Building Resilient Companies That Never Have to Bet the Farm

Originally posted on September 30, 2025.

The Unspoken Responsibility

When we think about the role of a founder, CEO, or president, we often picture someone relentlessly driving growth, chasing new opportunities, and pushing the business forward. But there is a hidden, essential responsibility beneath all that energy. One that often doesn't get enough attention.

Especially in family-owned businesses, where the stakes are multi-generational, survival must come before growth. One of the small business operator's foundational jobs is build a company that can't be easily destroyed by a single bad decision, unexpected event, or loss.

My overarching duty is to make sure I never put the company in a position where a single decision could jeopardize the company's existence. Resilience is not a constraint on growth; it's the foundation that makes sustainable growth possible.

Understanding Business Fragility

At the heart of business fragility is the concept of "single points of failure." These are critical dependencies within a company—maybe a client, employee, supplier, or system—that create existential risks.

Ironically, many of these vulnerabilities emerge from early successes. The big customer that put the company on the map or the founder's unique skills that drive early wins can become Achilles' heels if over-relied upon.

The paradox is clear: your greatest strengths can become your greatest vulnerabilities. For example, if a huge portion of your revenue depends on one client, you have gained a lot but also exposed yourself to devastating risk should that client leave. Similarly with a key supplier.

"Betting the company" on risky decisions should be forever off the table. CEOs must distinguish between smart risks and existential gambles that could topple everything they've built.

Where might you be vulnerable?

To protect the business, CEOs need to watch four main risk areas:

- Customer Concentration Risk: When
one client brings in over 20% of
revenue, or when the company
depends heavily on a single market or
region, the exposure is significant. I
lived this one in the early 2000s when
Nortel was over 30% of our book. We
grew like crazy at the time, but so did
they, and they stayed an overly large
proportion of our business. Until they
didn't.

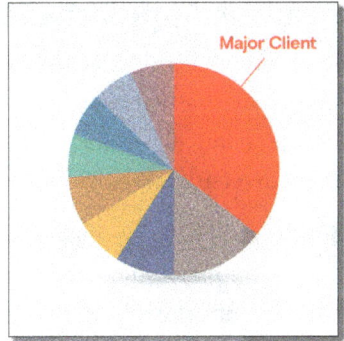

Major Client

- Key Person Risk: Founders, CEOs, or critical employees without
documented knowledge or succession plans create vulnerability. I once
took on a temporary role running a small manufacturer. They had a
single person on staff who knew how to design and quote the products,
and a single person on staff who could build them. None of the
management knew how to do any of this. Had either of these
individuals left for any reason, production and sales would have
screeched to a halt!

- Operational Dependencies: Relying on one supplier, facing technology
bottlenecks, or regulatory risks can disrupt business continuity. I was
part of a startup that built a proprietary device for those who fish but
don't own a boat with a fish finder. This was dependent on a single
supplier of custom technology, and that supplier had other customers
and product lines that were more strategic for them, often leaving us
high and dry.

- Financial Fragility: Dependence on one revenue stream or
overleveraging tied to a single contract can leave the company
financially unstable. So can overtrading or taking on a contract that's
too large for your current size. I was on the board of a company they
took a single contract that was almost equal to their annual revenue.
They couldn't support it financially, had to abandon it, and had a

severely damaged balance sheet.

Ok, there is a fifth area. Stupid decisions! You can make a bonehead decision in any area of your firm. That's why any big decision should be contemplated, and only after receiving counsel from as many viewpoints as possible.

Strategic Approaches to Risk Diversification

Managing these risks is an ongoing CEO responsibility. Early-stage companies often face unavoidable concentrations, and since they're small, every decision is large, relatively speaking. So they must be handled deliberately. As you grow, diversification—without losing core strengths—becomes vital.

Building resilient systems—like documented processes, cross-training, succession plans, financial buffers, and backup technology—is essential. Equally important is knowing when to say "no." CEOs need to weigh risk-adjusted returns and prioritize long-term resilience over short-term wins, even when tempting opportunities arise.

Original post URL: https://bradpoulos.com/dont-bet-the-farm/

A Big Company Strategy Tool Anyone Can Use

Originally posted on October 28 2025.

In 2007, I walked away from an industry I knew inside and out. I had the relationships, the expertise, and momentum such that everything looked perfect on paper. But I did a simple analysis that made me decide to carve a new path... The analysis used one of the strategy tools that we teach biz school students. While most suitably applied in a large corporate setting, they may have their place in the small business arena as well. The art is in knowing when to use which tool!

Small business owners often make critical decisions about expansion without understanding the deeper forces that determine success and profitability in that space. Michael Porter's Five Forces framework is a tool that any firm can use to assess the attractiveness (long-term prospects of profitability) of an industry. A five forces analysis is used mostly to inform decisions about market entry. It looks at the complete competitive landscape, not just your direct rivals, to reveal hidden threats and opportunities.

Porter's Five Forces

Developed by Harvard Business School professor Michael Porter in 1979, the Five Forces framework identifies five factors that determine whether an industry is attractive (profitable) or unattractive (difficult to make money in). Briefly, they are:

1. Competitive Rivalry – How intense is the competition among existing players?

2. Supplier Power – How much leverage do your suppliers have over pricing and terms?

3. Buyer Power – How much can customers demand lower prices or better service?

4. Threat of New Entrants – What barriers exist and how easy is it for new competitors to enter your market?

5. <u>Threat of Substitutes</u> – How "sticky" are customers and what alternative products or services could replace yours?

Interestingly, an attractive industry isn't necessarily one with few competitors. It's one where the combined forces allow businesses to maintain healthy profit margins. Look at the fast food industry. There are many competitors who thrive by carving out their own niche, product or location-wise.

A Real-World Decision Using Five Forces Analysis

In 2007, I faced a crossroads. My brother and I had spent ten years building a successful value-added reseller business in the wireless infrastructure space. We sold wireless equipment and installation/testing gear to telecommunications companies. When I left the company, I had a choice: start fresh in the same industry with the same customers and suppliers, or walk away entirely and do something else. On paper, it looked like the easy thing to do. I walked through an informal Five Forces analysis in my head. I never wrote it down, but I absolutely walked through the five forces like I'm going to do with you here:

Competitive Rivalry

Here we normally look at the number of competitors, how different their product offerings are, and how fast the industry is growing. If the pie is shrinking we will have to all duke it out for that diminishing pie. But if we all have different products, or the industry is growing really fast, we don't need to worry much about one another.

Want to follow along? Grab the Five Forces Worksheet from my website[5] and assess your industry as you read. In my case there were only a handful of direct competitors, who mostly got along. But it was a tiny industry with only four major customers and a bunch of small ones. We all served the same customers, and the real basis of competition was having an exclusive contract with one of the more well-known product lines. Add to that the fact that we all chased business from the same three large Canadian telcos, and that we were entering a brutal recession with zero growth prospects. Overall, this force was **negative**.

---

[5] *https://bradpoulos.com/wp-content/uploads/2025/10/Five-Forces-Analysis.pdf*

Supplier Power

Supplier and buyer power normally come down the relative size and number. When there are a large number of small suppliers, none of them have much power. A concentrated supplier base with larger players will have more power. Brand power and switching costs might also be relevant factors. As stated, we competed for the "good" lines, so our suppliers had a huge amount of power. They were massive corporations (billions in revenue) with brand names that our customers demanded. You served at the pleasure of your supplier with a 30-day termination clause. This one was **strongly negative**.

Buyer Power

It's relative size and number again. Buyer and supplier power are two sides of the same coin. The textbooks tell you to look at customer concentration, volume of purchases, switching costs, and price sensitivity, but I've yet to encounter a situation where it wasn't dominated by just how many and how big the buyers are. When there are many, individually, they have no bargaining power. Our company had three customers that mattered. Their volumes were significant to us, and while they had some switching costs it wasn't out of the question. They negotiated aggressively and had alternatives. Their power was indisputable. **Strongly negative.**

Threat of New Entrants

In general, the easier it is for a new company to enter an industry, the more negative we view an industry, all other things being equal. It's mostly about "barriers to entry". Think about a barbershop. There are limited capital requirements, no real benefits to be derived from economies of scale, easy access to necessary suppliers, no significant

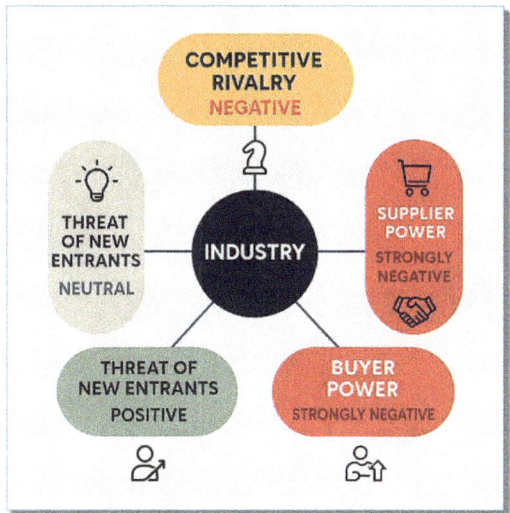

regulatory barriers, limited customer brand loyalty. This points to very low barriers. My business didn't have large capital requirements either, but you need established relationships with either suppliers OR customers (preferably both). Newcomers can't just waltz in and steal business. The barriers were relationship-based, not financial, and take years to build. This force was **positive**.

Threat of Substitutes

A substitute service or product is one that serves the same need as yours but in a fundamentally different way. Orange juice is a substitute for bottled water or ginger ale, not a competitor. We'd usually look at the price-performance trade-off and how easy it is to switch between the alternatives when examining this force.

While at the product level there are always substitutes, at the level of our firm, there really wasn't another way for our customers and our suppliers to meet. .

The world is full of middlemen, and we were one. At the time, anyway, there wasn't a realistic alternative, so no immediate threat, but also no advantage. This threat was **neutral**.

The Bottom Line

The scorecard didn't favour this industry. My one advantage stemmed from already being in the industry, so it wasn't really an industry force per se. The rest was at best neutral.

- Three forces: Strongly negative or negative
- One force: Positive
- One force: Neutral

I chose not to re-enter the industry. Interestingly, my brother continued, did so quite successfully, and eventually exited after many years. This highlights the importance of that one positive force, the industry relationships! That analysis saved me from a bad decision (for me). But you don't need to be at a crossroads to benefit from this tool. Here's how to apply it to your business...

What's in this for ME?

It's probably in every small business owner's interest to do a similar analysis to mine, just so you know where you stand. But where this is really helpful is where you're thinking about expanding your business into a new industry, or even new markets within your current industry. Ask these questions to yourself, then for each force, make an assessment as to where it lies on the continuum between strongly negative and strongly positive.

Competitive Rivalry

- How many direct competitors do I have in my market?
- Are our products/services truly differentiated, or are we all selling basically the same thing?
- Is the industry growing, flat, or shrinking?
- What are the primary bases of competition? (location, price, quality, service, innovation)
- Are there high fixed costs that force competitors to fight for volume?

▶ The red flags you want to look out for are many undifferentiated competitors, a shrinking market, or competition based mainly on price.

Supplier Power

- How many alternative suppliers could I use?
- How critical are my suppliers' products to my business?
- Could my suppliers easily sell direct to my customers?
- What are my switching costs if I change suppliers?
- Do my suppliers have much more market power than I do?

You lose power when there are only a few suppliers, no alternatives, or they could bypass you in the sales channel, and sell direct to your customers.

Buyer Power

- How concentrated are my customers? (Do a few accounts make up the majority of the revenue? Are any over 20% of the total?)
- How price-sensitive are they?
- How easy is it for them to switch to competitors?
- Do they have good information about costs and alternatives?
- Could they do what I do themselves (backward integration)?

If you have only a few large customers and a commoditized offering with low switching costs you have little power.

Threat of New Entrants

- How much capital does it take to start competing in my space?
- Do I have advantages from scale, proprietary technology, or brand?
- Are there regulatory requirements that protect me?
- How hard is it to access customers or distribution channels?
- Do customers have loyalty to established players?

✓ [6]The "green flags" you want to look for are high capital needs, strong brand advantages, regulatory barriers, and the need for established customer relationships. These make it harder for others to come into your sandbox!

- Threat of Substitutes
- What other solutions could address my customers' underlying need?
- Are there emerging technologies that could replace what I offer?
- What's the price-performance trade-off of substitutes vs. my offering?
- How willing are customers to switch to alternatives?

Keep an eye out for better and cheaper substitutes emerging. Changing customer preferences and low switching costs make this a credible threat.

Create Your Scorecard

Once you have rated each force, assess the overall attractiveness of the industry. If you score mostly negative forces, seriously reconsider entering this market unless you have a specific, defensible advantage. A mixed score is more likely. Here you want to focus your strategy on mitigating the biggest negatives and exploiting the positives. Obviously, if you score mostly positive forces, you've found a promising opportunity.

Actionable Strategies Based on Your Five Forces Analysis

Here are some ideas to incorporate into your strategy based on what the Porter five forces analysis tells you.

If Supplier Power is High:

- Diversify your supplier base and reduce dependence
- Develop alternative sources or in-house capabilities

---

[6] No, this was not created by AI. I actually put this in myself!

- Build stronger relationships with multiple suppliers
- Create more value for suppliers so they prioritize you
- Form buying groups with other businesses to increase leverage

If Buyer Power is High:

- Differentiate meaningfully so you're not just another vendor
- Create switching costs (loyalty programs, integration, specialized knowledge)
- Improve customer experience beyond the product itself
- Serve a broader customer base to reduce concentration risk
- Move up/down market to segments with less buyer power
- Add services that make you stickier

If Competitive Rivalry is Intense:

- Find your niche where you can dominate
- Differentiate on dimensions competitors can't easily copy
- Build brand equity that commands premium pricing
- Create cost advantages through efficiency or scale
- Focus on customer relationships rather than just transactions
- Consider whether to stay if the industry is fundamentally unattractive

⚠ When Not To Use It

- You're already IN the business (too late for entry analysis)
- The industry is in rapid transformation
- You're making tactical decisions (pricing, marketing)
- You're comparing yourself to specific competitors

If Threat of New Entrants is High:

- Build barriers through brand, relationships, or proprietary assets
- Create customer switching costs if possible
- Pursue exclusive partnerships with key suppliers or distributors
- Develop specialized expertise that's hard to replicate
- Build scale advantages that make it hard for small players to compete

If Threat of Substitutes is High:

- Monitor emerging alternatives constantly
- Innovate proactively rather than reactively
- Emphasize your unique advantages vs. substitutes
- Consider adopting the substitute yourself (if you can't beat them...)
- Bundle services that substitutes can't easily replicate

The goal isn't to find a perfect industry. The goal is to understand the battlefield so you can choose your battles wisely and develop strategies that actually work, given the forces you face. What industry forces are shaping your business?

Want a simple worksheet to guide your analysis?
https://bradpoulos.com/wp-content/uploads/2025/10/Five-Forces-Analysis.pdf

Original post URL: https://bradpoulos.com/porter-five-forces/

Change Management Isn't Optional — It's Survival

This guest post was written by Denise Fekete of Gore Mutual Insurance, and originally posted on November 1 2025.

We humans are innately resistant to change, even when it benefits us. Why? Fear of the unknown, a loss of control, our habitual nature, and fear of failure all play a role.

My thirty-plus-year career in the learning field has always aligned with driving change. Everything I do is about change. I love what I do, and in my work, I'm a change enthusiast! But that does not mean I am immune to resistance.

Take my golf game, for example. I had a goal to break a score of one hundred. I was so close in the spring, then an injury set me back. I nearly gave up playing altogether. When I returned, it felt like starting from scratch. Frustrated and disappointed, quitting seemed easier. But my social circle is full of golfers who would have given me a hard time if I walked away. So, I put in the physical and mental effort to get back in the game. The result? I broke one hundred in my final round of the year, whew!

My point: change takes effort. Simple. In our personal lives, we often choose the easy way out. But in our careers, that path can be risky, no matter your trajectory.

Try this: sit down and write out your resume, listing all the learning you have acquired in each role. You will see a great deal of change throughout your career, even if you are just starting out.

Every learning moment is a step toward opportunity, big or small. Did you resist any of it? Did that resistance help or hinder you?

Kübler-Ross Change Curve

When you reflect on the Kübler-Ross Change Curve, you can likely identify where you are, or have been, on that journey.

For example, when I joined my current organization, it was the perfect size:

small, well-known, great culture. Shortly after, a merger was announced. We would be moving from small to large in just a few years.

When I struggle with change, I lean on my Prosci Change Practitioner training, Cassandra Worthy's motivational insights, and the Kubler-Ross model to ground me. Looking at the curve, I saw my journey: shock at the announcement, questioning my reaction, sadness at the loss of what I had found. But having gone through two previous mergers, I quickly shifted to seeing the opportunities ahead. The merger is with another amazing organization, and I am now eager to get started. I have now moved into the decision and integration stages. I could have stayed in sadness and changed jobs, but it took effort to see the positives.

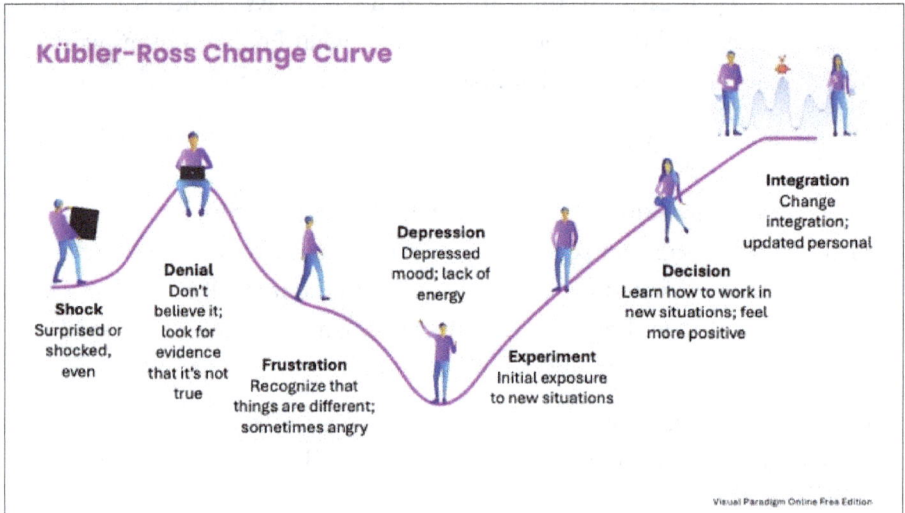

Kübler-Ross Change Curve

Shock Surprised or shocked, even

Denial Don't believe it; look for evidence that it's not true

Frustration Recognize that things are different; sometimes angry

Depression Depressed mood; lack of energy

Experiment Initial exposure to new situations

Decision Learn how to work in new situations; feel more positive

Integration Change integration; updated personal

Visual Paradigm Online Free Edition

There's a great scene in the film *Moneyball* where Brad Pitt's character addresses change with a scout. The movie, based on a true story, follows a baseball manager trying to build a team with limited funds. He partners with a baseball whiz kid whose ideas are met with resistance. One major staff member refuses to even consider the new approach. It's a powerful example of how humans instinctively resist change. In the end, the idea works and is now used by all major league teams.

Crossing the Chasm

Change is constant in today's workplace, which clashes with our fear of sudden shifts. If you are driving change, understanding its impact, on yourself and your collaborators, is critical.

Simon Sinek offers great insights into the human experience of change, and how to leverage early adopters to drive change internally.

His ideas align with the concept of Geoffrey Moore's *Crossing the Chasm*, which uses Rogers' *Diffusion of Innovation* curve to outline how people adopt new ideas or technologies:

- Innovators: Already onboard
- Early Adopters: Follow quickly
- Early Majority: Ask "What's in it for me?"
- Late Majority: Crossed the chasm but still need support
- Laggards: The most resistant and may never adopt

Resisters play a vital role in driving change. They surface opportunities and help ensure success.

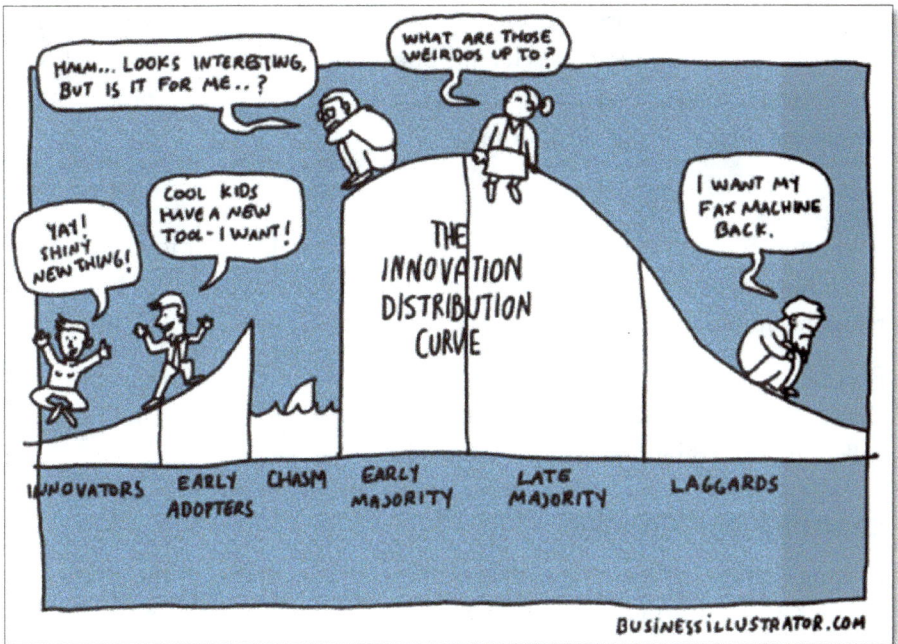

Leading Through Resistance: Driving Change Across the Chasm

This is where leaders play a critical role in driving change. One of your biggest challenges as a leader is helping others cross the chasm into the early majority, especially when you yourself haven't yet made that journey. This is exactly when your resistors will appear (if not sooner).

Resistors may show up as sadness, rejection, anger, uncertainty, or hyper-focus on what's wrong with the decision. As you deepen your understanding of change leadership, begin tracking which behaviors align with these reactions. This will help you later when identifying roles, assigning tasks, and building support systems.

Importantly, resistors aren't just obstacles, they're vital contributors. They often surface the tough questions, highlight overlooked risks, and bring hidden opportunities to light. They can lead the unsure and rally the likeminded. Their resistance, when acknowledged and engaged with empathy, can be a powerful force for success.

As a leader, your awareness of where you are on the change curve is essential, especially if you recognize yourself as a resistor. Managing your own mindset while driving change requires self-reflection. This reflection not only helps you understand your own reactions but also builds empathy for others navigating their own change journeys.

And remember, it's okay not to have all the answers. Let your team know you will follow up and make sure you follow up as that is a trust factor in relationship building.

Resistance is a signal, it means people are aware of and responding to the change. By building readiness early, you create space for meaningful dialogue, collaboration, and momentum.

Learning and Change

Driving change and learning should be closely tied together in the planning phase. Keeping learning fresh through change techniques helps people assimilate information and build confidence to adopt and adapt.

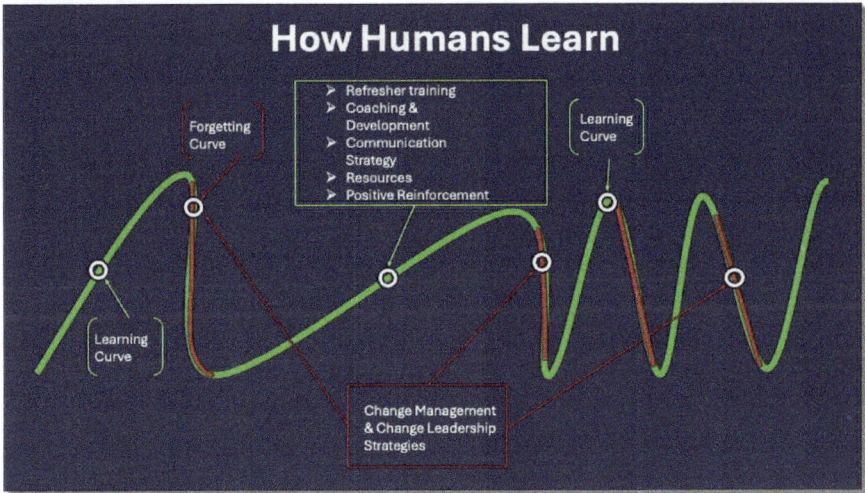

How Humans Learn

I recommend using *ADKAR*, the Prosci Change Management Model. It's simple and ensures a comprehensive plan to support change. Here's how you might use it in your small business. Imagine a small manufacturing business. The owner is trying to modernize but the old timers back in the shop push back on every sort of change, and don't want to even know what Excel is!

Awareness: The owner holds shop floor meetings explaining why modernization matters, not for her bottom line, but for job security, fewer frustrating errors, and staying competitive against larger manufacturers.

Desire: She connects the change to what workers care about: less overtime fixing mistakes, easier communication between shifts, and simpler processes. For the near retirees, she emphasizes legacy and helping train the next generation.

Knowledge: Training is hands-on, practical, and patient. No corporate training modules. Just real scenarios they faced daily. "Here's how you'd log that part shortage." or "Here's how you'd check the schedule for tomorrow."

Ability: She gives them time to practice without pressure. Mistakes are expected and normalized. The office manager is available for questions, no matter how basic.

Reinforcement: She celebrates small wins publicly to prevent backsliding. When the first digital inventory count matches the physical count, or when the first worker sends a successful shift handoff note. She also keeps the old paper backup system running for two months as a safety net, reducing anxiety.

Within six months, even the most resistant workers are using the system. Not enthusiastically, perhaps, but competently. And the business? It has reduced inventory errors by 40% and cut administrative time by hours each week.

Here is a sample of how it can be used in your planning.

ADKAR

Awareness Why	Desire What's in it for me (WIIFM)	Knowledge How will I/we use it?	Ability Support	Reinforcement Sustainment
I know and understand	I believe	I know how and when to...	I am able to...	I see the change is supported because...
How my performance is connected to success at XX company.	The plans support me to enhance my performance and potentially enable my career.	Use new terminology, navigate through the new process and use new technology and machines	Apply my new skills and knowledge to run the machinery confidently and identify any production issues.	My leaders provide me the opportunity to provide feedback with transparency to ensure processes and machinery are running to expectations.
Change Activities for each phase - Dependency is on complexity of changes				
➤ Communication Strategy ➤ Owner holds shop floor meeting to explain "The Why".	➤ Teaser video about the change ➤ In person sessions/townhalls to connect the WIIFM (What's In It For Me)	➤ Hands on practical training using machinery ➤ Resources for reference	➤Practicum sessions for safe learning with real scenarios to test knowledge	➤ Celebration of small wins ➤ Rewards and recognition ➤ Front line Feedback sessions to understand how the change is progressing

Change Management vs Change Leadership

Both are essential, but different and it is important to know the distinction. Here is a great video that explains the distinction.

Change is about stepping outside your comfort zone in a particular domain.

This pictorial shows how we move from the comfort zone, through fear and learning, to the growth zone. Can you see yourself in one of these zones based on any current changes in your world?

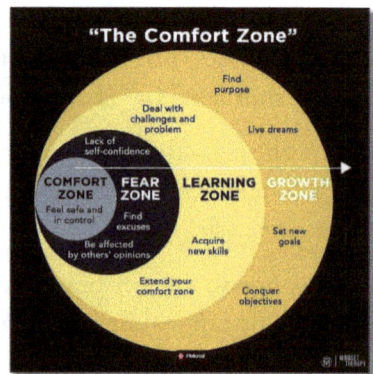

"The Comfort Zone"

I can! I am in the "Learning Zone", in the domain of building AI agents. It is interesting and engaging work. As a lifelong learner learning new skills motivates me. I use that energy to inspire my team to build their skills and knowledge to enable their growth. Role modeling for your team is an important thing to remember as a leader.

Change is a journey. If you approach it with a positive mindset, the adoption and adaption will be a more positive experience for everyone.

Denise Fekete is a senior Learning & Development strategist with deep expertise in human-centred learning design, AI innovation, change management, workforce transformation, and purpose-driven leadership. She brings a pragmatic approach to technology transformation, grounded in extensive experience across learning design, quality assurance, and change enablement. Denise has a proven track record of scaling learning programs through strategic use of technology and data, particularly within the insurance and financial services sectors.

Original post URL: https://bradpoulos.com/change-management/

Knowing Your Place: How to Visually Map Your Competition

Originally posted on November 8 2025.

Why You Need More Than a Gut Feel

Most small business owners think they know who their competition is. You probably do, if you're on your game. But if you're not sure, or you want to up your game in terms of how you think about your market and the players within it, here are two simple tools to help bring clarity to your competitive position.

We usually teach these as big company strategy tools, but you'll find both of them are also useful to the entrepreneur. Crystal clear competitive awareness can't be a bad thing. It will help you fine-tune your positioning in the industry, and take advantage of strategic gaps in the market.

The Competitive Matrix

A competitive matrix packs a lot of information into a small space. To do it right, you first need to understand how the game is played in your industry. Specifically, you need to identify the primary bases of competition. Most industries have between three and five non-negotiables; the things that you have to be good at to dominate an industry. These are the dimensions we will use to size up the competition.

And that's the next challenge. Identifying who your competitors are can also be tricky. Imagine that you're a used car dealer, specializing in middle-market, high-quality cars. You sell a lot of two-year old Hondas, the odd Infiniti or Lexus, and quite a few Volkswagen Jettas. Not far away is a "competitor" that only sells luxury used cars. Nothing below a BMW. Do you really compete? Do we even need to be good at the same things? Probably not!

You should probably narrow the scope of your competitive analysis to your segment of the used car industry, and consider the luxury specialists as a *substitute*. It doesn't mean we can't learn from them or we shouldn't study them, but we will confine the direct competitors to those who sell what we do.

Let's say the key success factors for this industry are:

- Access to inventory: Since they don't manufacture their product they have to be good at sourcing it.
- Competitive Pricing Strategy: Margins are tight in this kind of business so your profit will come from velocity which means you need to be competitive on price.
- Customer Trust & Reputation: The used car industry has a lot of warts on it from a customer perspective. Any ability to establish a good reputation is going to be a durable differentiator.
- Digital Presence & Lead Generation: Nowadays most used car buyers start online so visibility and digital conversion are now paramount.
- Operational Excellence: In a low-margin business, you need to be good at all of the little things to be profitable (upselling, inventory management, reconditioning, delivery, regulatory compliance).

The first two of these can be somewhat difficult to ascertain, but the others are not. The competitive matrix might look something like what we see below. This version includes weighting for each of the factors.

	Weight	Us		Competitor 1		Competitor 2	
		Rating	Score	Rating	Score	Rating	Score
Inventory	25%	9	2.25	8	2.0	6	1.5
Pricing	25	7	1.75	10	2.5	8	2.0
Reputation	20	9	1.8	9	1.8	7	1.4
Leads	15	8	1.2	8	1.2	8	1.2
Excellence	15	7	1.05	8	1.2	8	1.2
Total			8.05		8.7		7.3

The matrix shows how you stack up on an overall basis, and where you stand on each key factor. But it treats all competitors as if they're playing variations of the same game. Some dealers may be running completely different business models, and that's where our second tool comes in.

The Strategic Group Map

The Strategic Group Map is about how businesses cluster, often based on similar models or strategic approaches. It's a highly visual tool that helps you see what strategy the various players in an industry are following, and may point to opportunities to carve out a different strategy, opening up a "blue ocean" for your firm.

We use a graphical 2x2 grid comparing businesses along two non-correlated competitive dimensions. For example you might choose price/quality as one dimension and the breadth of their operations as another. Firms that have in-house mechanic, body shop, detailing, and financing operations would be at one end of the continuum, and simple car lots that farm out virtually everything beyond a quick vacuuming at the other.

It's important that the axes for the comparison be non-correlated (hence us grouping price and quality as a single one), otherwise you'll end up with a straight line and won't really learn anything. It's also important that the two axes actually matter competitively. They have to influence how businesses win or lose, otherwise who cares? They may or may not be customer-facing.

The map is created by plotting the various competitors (or groups of them) using circles that represent their relative sizes.

In our fictitious example, it seems there may be an opportunity to compete with a mid-

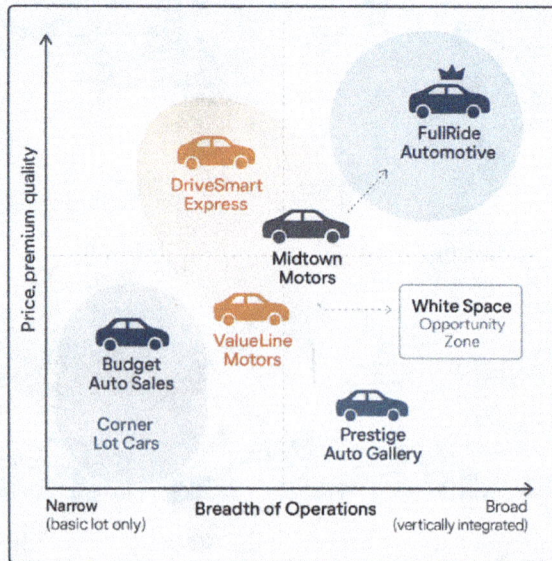

- 142 -

price/broad operations focus.

You can't beat every competitor, and you don't need to. You just need to know which ones actually matter, and who is playing what variation of the game.

Original post URL: https://bradpoulos.com/competitive-mapping

LEGAL, FINANCE & OWNERSHIP

Beyond the P&L: Why the Cash Flow Statement Should Be Every Small Business Owner's Obsession

Originally posted on June 13, 2025.

As someone who's been involved in business and side hustles since my teen years, understanding the P&L has always come naturally. Expenses, revenue, and profit; they're all terms we use in everyday language. So when a small business owner looks at a P&L for the first time, it probably makes immediate sense. It just clicks.

The Balance Sheet is equally intuitive. Most people get the gist of what they own, what they owe, and what's left over. It's the kind of stuff that even comes up when you're talking about mortgages or car loans.

But the Statement of Cash Flows doesn't have a common, simple analogy to our daily lives. I didn't truly appreciate it until my MBA, and even then, it wasn't until I managed cash flow firsthand that I realized just how critical it is to business survival. Especially as a planning tool.

It's arguably the most important report of all the statements.

If it doesn't jingle,
it doesn't count.
- Jim Hatch (Ivey Business School)

The quote is from my MBA finance prof, Jim Hatch.

The concept that cash is king is so vitally important that on the first day of any finance course I give I write the question, with the two blanks, and then

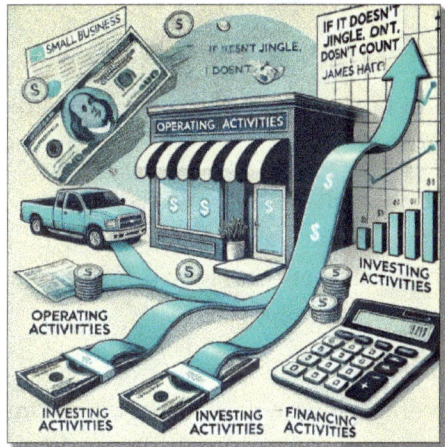

fill them in. Then I would tell them that this would be the bonus question on the final exam.

And then tell them again in every class!

Why the P&L Misleads

You're showing a profit but your bank account tells a different story. What's going on?

Many small business owners have experienced this: the P&L looks great, but you're worried about covering payroll or paying suppliers. It's like having a fitness tracker that says you burned 500 calories today, and you're about to pass out from hunger.

The reason is simple: the P&L measures profitability, not cash. And while profit is important, it doesn't mean much if you don't also have liquidity. If you're growing, cash will almost always lag profits. As a result, you will often have cash flow issues that the cash flow statement can help you to understand. It can, in fact, help to predict them—and then avoid them.

Profit ≠ Cash: Profit is malleable. Depreciation, bad debt allowances, and revenue timing can all distort it. A small business owner can make profit appear better or worse simply by adjusting spending or accounting methods, but none of that will change the underlying cash situation.

> *"In a small company, profit is whatever the owner says it is."*
> *—Brad Poulos*

The CFS, by contrast, cuts through the noise. It gives you a clean view of where money is piling up, or leaking out. Details that you won't see in your P&L.

Cash Doesn't Lie: The Statement of Cash Flows

The Statement of Cash Flows or Cash Flow Statement (CFS) simply tracks how cash actually moves through your business. It organizes inflows and outflows into three broad categories that represent the three major functions or activities of any organization:

Operating Cash Flow

This is the cash generated (or used) by your core business activities. It includes all sales and expenses but also balance sheet changes like purchases of inventories, or payments from customers and to suppliers. This section will add any non-cash expenses like depreciation/amortization because these are "expenses" but don't involve a cash outlay.

Operating Cash Flow should normally be positive in what I call a Normal Healthy Growing Company (or NHGC), which is a business that's profitable, generating positive operating cash flow, and reinvesting in itself at a sustainable pace.

If your core operations aren't spinning off positive cash, you're either funding losses through loans, burning through reserves, or selling off assets to pay the bills. None of these are sustainable.

Positive operating cash flow is the financial heartbeat of a healthy business. It proves that the business model works, and that growth is being driven by actual performance, not by borrowing or asset sales.

Investing Cash Flow

When a company "invests" we mean investing in long-term or fixed assets that will be used to generate revenue in the business. This includes items like equipment, vehicles, computers, or real estate. These transactions don't happen every day, but they're critical for growth and strategic direction. So if this section shows negative cash flow, it is generally a good sign. It means you're investing in the future of the business. If it's consistently positive, it may indicate you're selling off assets—potentially a red flag, depending on the context.

Financing Cash Flow

Financing activities capture the cash moving in or out of your business from lenders, investors, or owners. This includes taking out loans, repaying debt, injecting owner capital, or paying dividends. If you see cash flowing into the business here, it might mean you're taking on debt or raising capital. If it's flowing out, you're repaying loans or distributing profits.

How to Read the Statement (Without Falling Asleep)

Watch this line: "Net Increase (or Decrease) in Cash" or "Net Cash Flow." This number explains the change in your actual bank balance over the reporting period. If your business isn't constantly lighting your hair on fire and your net cash flow is regularly positive, you've earned the right to unclench, at least a little. Look at bit deeper to reveal whether your business is heading in the right direction. If your operating cash flow is strong and consistently positive, that's the ideal scenario.

But if it's negative, that's a major red flag. It means your business operations are consuming more cash than they're generating, and *someone* is financing losses. You need to investigate and act quickly. Find out why your operations are consuming cash. Do you have a healthy gross profit margin? If so, look at working capital. You may be slow collecting or overdoing inventory levels.

Conversely, a negative cash flow from investing activities is a good sign. It means that you're buying equipment or assets to support future growth. On the other hand, if you're consistently showing positive investing cash flow, it might mean you're selling off business assets just to stay afloat.

The biggest concern arises when you see positive financing cash flow combined with negative operating cash flow. That combination usually indicates you're borrowing just to keep the lights on. It's not a sustainable model and should trigger immediate attention.

What a Small Business Operator to Do?

Review your Cash Flow Statement every month, not just at tax time. Then use it to ask better questions like: Are we generating cash from operations? Are we collecting from customers fast enough? Are we investing ahead of our means? Then take action. Chase overdue invoices. Trim excess inventory. Delay spending that's not urgent. Renegotiate supplier terms. All of it shows up in the cash flow statement—you just have to look.

Budgeting with the Cash Flow Statement:

When you budget using all four key financial statements, including the CFS, you gain the ability to forecast future cash crunches or surpluses. A good budget is monthly, not annual, and it doesn't just estimate revenue and expenses. It tracks when money will actually move—including loan payments, capital purchases, inventory buys, and owner draws.

Here's what a smart budget framework includes:

- **P&L (Income Statement):** Measures revenue and expenses over time.

- **Statement of Retained Earnings:** Shows how profits are split between reinvestment and distributions to owners.

- **Balance Sheet:** A point-in-time snapshot of what you own, what you owe, and what's left for the owners.

- **Cash Flow Statement:** Breaks down cash movement during a period across operating, investing, and financing activity.

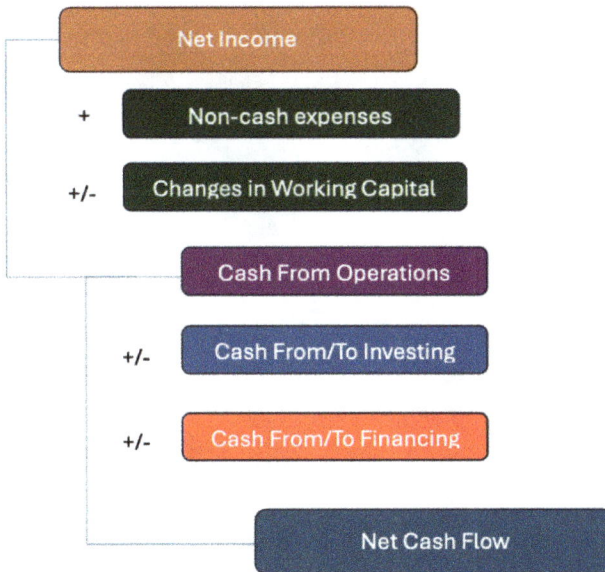

Together, these statements give you a full picture of your business's financial condition. But it's the CFS that shows what's really going on with your cash, which is what keeps the lights on.

You don't need to be an accountant to do this. My website has an Excel planning tool that will allow you to create a 3-year budget and financial statements without knowing any accounting[7].

If you'd like a more in depth explanation of the cash flow statement, check

---

[7] *https://bradpoulos.com/business-resources*

out this article on appeconomyinsights.com:
https://www.appeconomyinsights.com/p/how-to-analyze-a-cash-flow-statement.

Original post URL: https://bradpoulos.com/cash-flow-statement/

Alternative to Minority Shareholder In Small Private Companies

Originally posted on June 14, 2021.

Minority Shareholder? Doesn't Make Sense in A Small Company

I can't count the number of times I've had the discussion with friends, colleagues, students, or clients about issuing, selling, or optioning shares of a small private company to key employees and creating a new class of minority shareholder.

If the company is destined for great things...

a likely IPO/RTO or strategic purchase by another firm, and there's a clear path and *intent* to a liquidity event within no more than 5 years, then ok, sure. But if you're just trying to build a good solid business for the long term, don't do it!

You'll save yourself a mountain of future headaches, and your employee some grief as you'll spare them the sad reality of what being a minority shareholder in a small private company really means.

For the purposes of this discussion, I'm going to relay a real situation from about 15 years ago when I was growing mmWave Technologies with my brother. To protect the guilty, I will just call this person "Dave". Dave was a key player in our company, holding the title of VP of Sales and the responsibility for a significant portion of our overall business. Dave was also the kind of person who was obsessed with what other people had.

[Sidenote: We were out for a nice dinner; just us two. I told him that a salesperson at one of our suppliers had just received a $400K bonus. He literally squeezed his wine glass so hard that he broke it, spilling red wine over the table. Dave was really high-strung and cared a lot about what others got!]

So it was inevitable that he would come looking for "a piece of the rock". At the time of our discussion, he wanted to buy 5% of the company which would have resulted in four shareholders, three of which owned the other 95% equally. The following is the discussion – more or less – that we had over this, as I tried to talk him out of the idea of being a minority shareholder.

Ok, so you'd like to get a piece of the rock, eh?! (Become a Minority Shareholder)

Let's talk about why. There are practical and emotional or ego-driven reasons. I can't deal with the latter. In terms of practical reasons, there are really three reasons that you'd want to own shares in a company of mine, and I will address each one.

1. You want more influence on company direction.

First, you're already a VP, and the highest paid non-owner in the company. We talk every day about key issues and you're as consulted as any of the owners ALREADY on key day-to-day issues. As a 5% shareholder, you'd theoretically have 5% "say" on a handful of things, which as a practical matter is about equivalent to ZERO percent say. You can't even influence a vote or combine your, uh, *power (?)*, with another shareholder because 5% on top of 31.7% doesn't amount to diddly.

Even if it did, what would you get "say" over?

Well, under the Canada Business Corporations Act, you get to decide a few things. First, you get to pick the auditor, except we don't do an audit, so that's meaningless. You also get to vote on the directors of the company and any other really big decisions. So as a practical matter, you've already got the exact amount of influence over this company that you're going to get, and you didn't need to buy shares to get it!

2. You want to participate in profits each year.

Ok, so I assume you mean "dividends" since you already take part in the management bonus program and the profit sharing program. Since we started the company in 1991, the grand total of all dividends ever paid by this company is (drum roll please), ZERO! It's not tax efficient for us to declare and pay dividends, so we never do. There's no benefit for you here.

3. You want to cash in when the company gets sold.

Well the problem is, Davey, we aren't *planning* on selling any time soon, so I'd hate to see you invest your money and then have to wait years or decades to see any return.

However just in case, since this is the only real point you've made so far, how about we set up a phantom share plan for you and a few other key managers, so we can share the spoils if we ever do sell? It gives you all the benefits of owning shares without having to make any investment.

And the truth is, that's the best option for situations like this. A *Phantom Share Plan* allows you to tailor exactly how you will compensate senior people as the company grows, pays dividends, or gets sold. It costs employees nothing, is a lot easier to set up than an Employee Share Ownership Plan, and eliminates all the issues that come with minority shareholders like what do you do if they quit or get fired, and how much to charge them for the shares (if you say you're going to give them away I will take you off my LinkedIn!).

It's obviously something you need to consult with your legal advisors on, but a great alternative to creating a bunch of small, minority shareholders. If you need help with this, reach out.

I should loop back to the case for those who DO plan to have an exit or liquidity event. In that case you do NOT want a phantom share plan. Rather you should have either an Employee Share Ownership Plan that allows all of your employees to buy shares, or an Option Plan that provides options to some or all employees.

Oh... and what did Dave say to our suggestion that we give him part of the company when and if we sold it?

He quit!

Original post URL: https://bradpoulos.com/management/minority-shareholder/

Should I Incorporate My Business?

Originally posted on August 26, 2021.

In short, probably, Yes!

Clients criticize me sometimes for not being more directive. For laying out the pros and cons and then telling them to decide. So this time I will invoke what one of my old bosses used to call the "right answer theorem". And the right answer is *yes*, you should incorporate your small business.

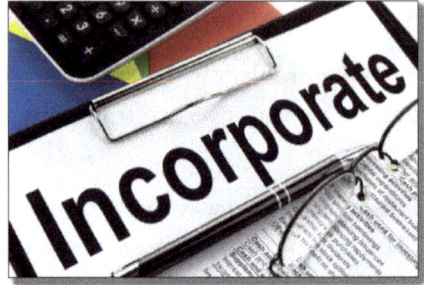

I should clarify... my audience is *small* and medium-sized business owners, not *micro*-businesses. As I write, I'm assuming that you have already made the plunge into entrepreneurship and you have:

- a bunch of customers;
- revenues of at least $1MM;
- some employees; and
- some assets, both the company and personally.

With that in mind, if you're asking the question, "Should I Incorporate My Business", then you probably should. A quick search on the web of this question will no doubt find you a balanced Pro vs Con analysis of this question, with the pros normally beating the cons by a hair, Honestly, what utter bullshit! The Pros absolutely murder the Cons in most cases.

I'm not going to fill this post with material about the characteristics of the various forms of company organization – sole proprietorships, partnerships, co-operatives, and corporations – but will rather assume the reader knows the basics already and needs to understand which one fits their situation best. I'm also going to skip the co-op since the business' purpose often is what leads to the choice of that form.

So which form makes the most sense in your case?

Sole Proprietor

Absolutely the simplest and easiest way to start a company, the sole proprietorship really only applies for the *smallest of businesses*, with relatively modest needs for capital, assets, and employees. Many businesses start here and then quickly move on to incorporation, however, a freelancer or micro-business owner may continue to use this form indefinitely. But really, only them. The kicker here is the unlimited liability that comes with this form of ownership. The fact that there's no legal separation between the company and the owner means that they are on the hook personally for anything that happens in that company. Saving a few bucks on incorporation costs (or even taxes!) just isn't worth this risk.

General Partnership

Almost as simple as the sole proprietorship, partnerships are formed upon the agreement of one or more partners. Normally this should be enshrined in a partnership agreement but it need not be. The partnership's *name* will have to be registered with the government (unless you only use the names of the partners, e.g., Brad Poulos and Steve Stevens) but otherwise, it takes no red tape to set up. Like the sole proprietor, the General Partners (GP) in a partnership are personally liable for the debts of the partnership. Both jointly and severally. So when one partner messes up it's possible the other partner or partners, especially if they have deeper pockets, will be on the hook. That alone should steer you toward the corporation.

Limited Partnership

A Limited Partnership differs from the General Partnership in that a Limited Partnership can have both General Partners (at least one) who is responsible for running the business day-to-day, and is liable for any debt of the business, as well as Limited Partners (LP) who are not involved in the operation, and as a result whose liability is limited to their investment.

Limited Liability Partnership

Certain professions can take advantage of a Limited Liability Partnership (LLP). The rules around LLPs vary greatly throughout Canada and the US. In Ontario, LLPs are permitted provided that the profession is governed by an Act that allows an LLP to practice as a profession (for example, in the case of midwives, it is the Midwifery Act, 1991, for accountants it is the Public Accounting Act, 2004). If you fall into this category, an LLP makes very good sense.

Corporation

Why not incorporate your Small Business???

I'm going to go in reverse order here and lay out the normal arguments against corporations, debunk them, and then make the case for the corp as the go-to, default, automatic, choice. Of course, there are exceptions.

Costs

This one is a real laugher. The costs are:

- the cost of incorporation itself which is $200 for a DIY online incorporation in Ontario, or around $500 if you have a professional like a paralegal do it for you;
- "costs" associated with filling out and filing forms, which as far as I know is one form per year with a filing fee of $12 that takes 5 minutes to complete online;
- lawyer's or paralegal fees for a shareholders' agreement, which implies more than one owner, so in that case, you'd still want a partnership agreement and the cost is the same as a shareholders' agreement;
- the cost of filing taxes, which might be slightly higher than with the sole proprietor and is likely the same as filing taxes under a partnership.

Not a very compelling argument for putting everything you own at risk.

Taxes

At low revenue and profit levels, it's possible that you'd pay less tax if you didn't incorporate, but as revenues and profits rise, the flexibility in tax strategies offered by a corporation will be much greater. If you plan to stay small and have limited profits, why do you read this blog??

Increased Complexity and Paperwork

Also a bit of a laugh. Most of the paperwork demanded by the federal, regional, provincial/state and municipal governments is a result of the *business*, not because it's a corporation. Payroll filings, sales tax payments and filings, and other compliance documents are required regardless of the form of organization.

Eliminates Ability To Represent Oneself in Federal Court

This is from a paralegal friend of mine:

One downside of being incorporated instead of being a sole proprietor is that you cannot represent yourself in Federal Court without permission from a judge. Your business could suffer a default judgment if it can't afford the legal fees that even baseless claims can cost.

Should I Incorporate My Business?

Now the compelling arguments in favor of incorporating.

Limited Liability

This is where it begins and ends with me. Hands down, the big advantage to incorporating is the limited liability offered to the owners of the incorporated company. The corporation is a separate legal entity from the owners, unlike the sole proprietorship or partnership, so a debt of the company is not necessarily a debt of the owner. The term "limited" liability means that an individual shareholder's liability is no greater than *the amount they have invested in the company*. You can still lose everything you invest, but unless you've signed something to the contrary, no one can come after your house, car, boat, or firstborn child.

Raising Capital

It's illegal to sell even a part of yourself, so raising capital in a sole proprietorship is very difficult. Nigh on impossible unless you are using the capital to purchase physical assets. A corporation can borrow money, or issues shares, in order to obtain additional capital for expansion *in its own right*.

Income Splitting and Tax Deferral

Another huge advantage of the corp is the ability to split income with family members and plan for future events like retirement or the death of the founder. Corporations pay a different tax rate than individuals, and dividends have different tax treatment than salary or bonuses. Plus a spouse paid a salary by the company has a lower marginal tax rate than their spouse who is taking a larger salary from the company. Your tax accountant can use these facts to determine the best mix of company profit, bonuses, and dividends paid to the various family members and can minimize the overall tax burden at the family level, leaving greater wealth for future generations.

Continuity and Estate Planning

When the sole proprietor of a business dies, the business dies with them. The assets of the business would be distributed based on the owner's will, and while it is possible for the business to continue, it can be tricky to reconstruct it under a different individual or a corporation. If that same owner had simply set up a corporation, the business would not die with them. It would still have assets, a bank account, employees, customers, and loans. I would just have a new owner based on the instructions in the deceased owner's will. The business would carry on as before, with the obvious disruption that would come from the loss of a key person, and most likely its top leader.

Credibility

Having the Limited, Ltd., Inc., Corp, Corporation, or other designation following your company name implies a certain level of sophistication that lends credibility.

So the answer to the question, "Should I incorporate my business?" is probably yes.

This brings up the question of whether you should incorporate federally or provincially. I usually default to Federal. If you are planning on operating or doing business in more than one province, I would go with Federal. You still need to register in each province if you're going to do business there, but you will have guaranteed use of your business name by virtual of the federal registration.

If you're in doubt contact your lawyer, paralegal, other trusted advisor or me.

Original post URL: https://bradpoulos.com/should-i-incorporate-my-business/

2/10, Net-30 Is Financially Illiterate. Here's Why.

Originally posted on June 2, 2025.

Or: Why You Might Be Paying 36% Interest to Get Your Own Money Faster

"Cash flow is king," they say.

But what if I told you that one of the most common ways businesses try to improve it, by offering early payment discounts like 2/10; Net-30, is basically giving out high-interest loans... to your customers?

And I'm not being dramatic. I'm talking 36.7% annualized interest. That's loan-shark territory. All for the pleasure of getting paid 20 days sooner.

Let's break this down.

What is 2/10; Net-30?

It's shorthand on an invoice that means:

"You get a 2% discount if you pay me within 10 days. Otherwise, I expect full payment in 30 days."

Sounds innocent. Even helpful. You're giving your customer a little carrot to pay faster. Maybe you've even been *taught* this is good business practice. I used to teach finance at Humber College and my (accountant) colleagues taught this as if it was a routine, beneficial practice.

Spoiler alert: It's not. At least not for most small businesses.

Do the Math, Then Pick Your Jaw Off the Floor

Let's say you invoice a client for $10,000. Normally, they pay in 30 days. You offer them a 2% discount if they pay in 10 days. That saves them $200 and costs you the same.

So you get $9,800 instead of $10,000. And you get it 20 days earlier. Not bad, right?

Wrong!

The annualized cost of that $200 "cash advance" is a whopping 36.7%.

Thirty. Six. Point. Seven. Percent.

You could get a short-term business loan or a line of credit for a third of that cost. Hell, your personal credit card is only 1/2 as expensive.

How is it so expensive? Here's the math...

The customer is paying 20 days early. You need to process that in your brain as a 20-day loan. They're technically not obligated to pay you

$$\frac{2\%}{20\,days} = \frac{0.1\%}{day} = \frac{36,5\%}{per\ year}$$

the money for another 20 days, so they are "loaning" you the money. The cost of that loan is 2% for 20 days, or 0.1%/day. Multiply that by 365 and you get a jaw-dropping 36.5% annual cost.

It's actually worse! If you compound it, it's 44%.

$(1 + 0.001)^{365} = 1.44$

Why are you borrowing money at rates twice what a credit card charges a high-school student?

What Should You Do Instead of Prepayment Discounts

If you're using early payment discounts to smooth out your cash flow, there are better ways:

Invoice factoring or discounting: Sell your receivables to a third party. Yes, you'll pay a fee, but it'll likely be way less than 36%. Bonus: they can take on the collection risk.

Tighter credit policy: Don't wait 60 days for chronic late payers. Set expectations up front and enforce them. Become a pain in their behinds! Automated follow-ups the day after sending the invoice, and then 10 and 3 days before payment is due, can do wonders.

Use Deposits and Milestone Payments: For project-based work, bill upfront or in chunks. No need to offer a discount when you're already holding a portion of the cash.

When Might a Discount Make Sense?

To be fair, sometimes it's the best of bad options. It's ok if every once in a while, you *have to!*

- You're in a liquidity crunch, and fast cash matters more than margins. Sometimes time is tight and options are limited. As long as this is something you do only here and there, there's little harm in it.
- If you've got massive margins and these terms accelerate a lot of volume, the math might work (the key here is to DO the math!).
- The customer always pays early, and you've priced it in.
- You're trying to hit a liquidity target or sweeten a key relationship.
- You've got fat margins and this accelerates big volumes that bring scale advantages.

So there are definitely times it's ok, but it should be intentional, not automatic.

Final Word: Be a Banker, but On Purpose!

You wouldn't borrow money at 36% interest to fund your business. But, would you *invest* it at that rate? Would you lend your supplier money at that rate?

In other words, when it comes to these discounts...

"Would I take this deal if the roles were reversed?"

If you're the one receiving a 2/10, Net-30 offer, you should practically sprint to your chequebook. Why? Because taking that 2% discount for paying 20 days early is the equivalent of earning a 36.7% annualized return. If you have enough payables and are cash rich, you can earn a nice return just on the entirely risk-free activity of paying your bills early.

Do you earn a 36.7% return on the other assets that are in use at your firm? Does your retirement account earn that. Remember, it's a RISK-FREE investment! You're getting paid to do something that you were going to do anyway, pay your bill. It's better than almost anything legal.

So yes, as a seller, you may want to think twice. But as a buyer? Take the deal. Every time.

If you're contemplating a different discount structure and want to know the cost, download my easy-to-use Excel Prepayment Discount Cost Calculator to plug in your own terms and see what you're really giving away (https://bradpoulos.com/business-resources/#prepayment).

Looking for Additional Resources?

Better Cash Flow Management Tools

FundThrough (Invoice Factoring for Small Business)
https://www.fundthrough.com/

Float (Cash Flow Forecasting Software)
https://www.floatapp.com/

Small Business Financial Resources

BDC's guide to managing cash flow in Canada: bdc.ca/guide

Canadian government advice on financing growth: ised.canada.ca/research

Want to better understand why you feel poor despite growing sales? Check out the next post about cash flow issues.

Original post URL: https://bradpoulos.com/prepayment-discounts/

Cash Flow Issues. Or, Why Growing Businesses Always Feel Broke

Originally posted on May 30, 2025.

...And what Smart Owners Do About It

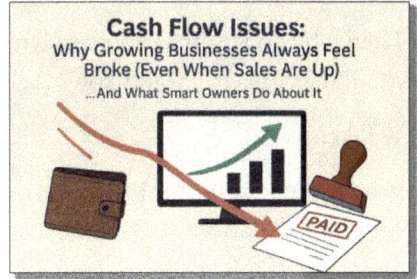

Who Knew? Growth Can Kill!

"Cash flow is king," they say.

Anyone with even a modicum of business experience knows there are a dozen ways to go under:

- Ruthless competitors
- Losing a key customer
- The founder's idiot kid takes over, torching the legacy

And at the end of the day, almost all of them show up as cash flow issues.

Digging deeper, consider these two paradoxical realities. They don't teach these in business school.

You can grow yourself right out of business.
---

and

If you want your company to actually throw off some cash to the owners...
Slow down the growth.

The Paradox of Growth - Cash Flow Issues Begin!

Your company is on fire.

- Twenty-four straight months of sales growth.
- Double the size you were three years ago.
- People, revenue, energy are all up.

You just told your spouse the company had a record-breaking month.

Then why do you find yourself lying awake that same night, wondering if you'll make payroll tomorrow?

WTAF?

Why is every indicator going up, except your bank balance?

Most of us get that growth takes resources. If you're already running a lean operation with no idle staff or unused space, then scaling up means adding capacity. That might be more salespeople, another location, more equipment, or extra techs and tools, depending on your business.

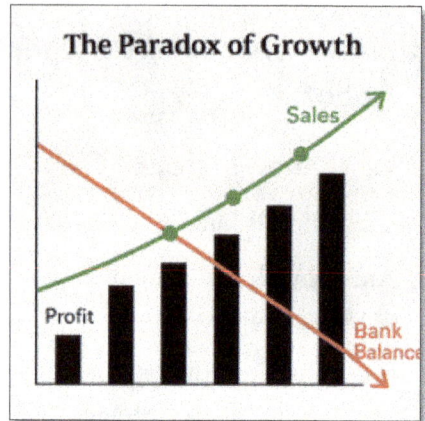

The Paradox of Growth

And of course, all of that takes money. Time-wise, revenues always lag expenses.

Where the Cash Really Goes

It's not just fixed assets like vans, and furniture and gear that suck up money. Often we overlook working capital. That means:
Inventory: You're stocking up ahead of sales.

Receivables: You're acting as a bank while customers pay you in 30-60 days.

Float: You simply need more daily cash to keep the machine running.

Companies have two basic ways to fund growth: internal or external.

Internal

Reinvested profits: Retaining earnings instead of distributing them to shareholders allows you to fund growth directly from operations.

Working capital optimization: Freeing up cash by reducing inventory levels, collecting receivables faster, or delaying payments to suppliers without harming operations.

External

Debt: Bank financing, invoice factoring, asset-based lending, leases, purchase order financing. Any external funding that will be repaid.

Equity: Raising funds by bringing in new investors or having existing owners contribute additional capital in exchange for shares in the company.

How I Learned about Overtrading

This is an excerpt from my book, The Small Business Operator's Manual.

> This happened about 2003.
>
> I will never forget the day the bank manager called me to tell me that we were doing great, and the bank was pleased to see us growing so fast with such an "A-player" customer list, so therefore the owners would have to put more money into the company.
>
> I was like... WTF?
>
> He explained that as we had grown so quickly, our working capital needs had outstripped the ability of the company to generate new cash. Up to that point, the difference was being made up by a bank loan. But he had decided as of that moment that it was our turn. He said to me, "Come on, Brad. We both know you're overtrading."
>
> He assumed I was familiar with the term, given that I had an MBA. I was not. However, I was armed with Google (although at that time, it was probably Alta Vista!), so I quickly pulled up the definition: "...the practice of conducting more business than can be supported by a firm's working capital."
>
> The bank manager was concerned because when this happens, a company can run out of cash and ultimately go bankrupt. Banks don't like their customers going bankrupt, especially when they are owed money by them!
>
> I promised to talk to my partners and get back to him, which, by the way, I never did. I never heard from him again about this, but it was a wake-up call to manage cash a lot more tightly for the time being.
>
> And THAT is how I learned what overtrading was!

It's also how I learned that sometimes you can ignore the bank when they try to tell you what to do (at least until they ask the second time).

Even if you're not overtrading, fast growth can make it very difficult to manage cash flow. Smart owners understand (and plan For) it. They watch cash like a hawk. They don't delegate this unless it's to a highly capable and conscientious individual. Running out of cash means your company comes to a halt.

How do I stay sane (and solvent) and minimize the bite of cash flow issues resulting from rapid growth?

Knowledge is power.

You have to run at least a 13-week rolling cash flow forecast.

The template[8] on my website runs for 52 weeks, but can be used for any time period. You want to know well in advance if you're going to have a cash crunch so you can manage around it, either by getting customers to pay early or arranging extended terms with one or more suppliers.

Stay tight on your receivables. Treat your collections as critical. Now is not the time to let customers begin stretching you.

Review your inventory levels and consider whether you can reduce them without incurring a significant risk of lost sales due to low stock levels. Inventory management is an art, and an area often neglected in smaller firms. Every $ of inventory you don't buy is a $ of financing you don't have to source!

Are your costs, and hence, your margins, optimized? Can you raise prices without losing a meaningful amount of business?

All of these will throw off a bit of extra cash. If you foresee a potentially serious cash shortfall, first look at internal sources of cash. Can you manage your working capital better?

After that, you need to consider either putting extra funds into the company personally or obtaining bank or other financing. As a short-term option, factoring or accounts receivable financing might work. They're a bit expensive

---

[8] https://bradpoulos.com/business-resources/#CashFlowPlanning

but very flexible and relatively easy to set up if you have high-quality receivables (not aged; good customers).

Pro Tip! Any $ you put into the company should be recorded as a shareholder loan. If you have a bank loan, they may push you to put in equity. Resist.

Another Pro Tip! Resist any ideas you might have about selling shares to an employee to solve a cash problem. The post on page XX and my book *The Small Business Operator's Manual* both provide more detailed explanations of why this is a bad idea.

What not to do:

Don't offer prepayment discounts. The cost of the money is too high. This will be covered in a future blog post, so please look here for a more detailed explanation.

One final "watch out"

High growth can be a lot of fun, and if managed well can literally transform your business by taking it to the next level in your industry. But high growth has to be accompanied by healthy margins. Thin margins + fast growth = bankruptcy waiting to happen

Cash flow issues are a part of any business. Consider sleepless nights a rite of passage for the serious entrepreneur. And take some comfort in this widely-cited quote, of unknown origin:

> *"Revenue is vanity, profit is sanity, but cash is king."*

Want to Actually Take Money Out of the Business? Slow Down!

As we've seen, if you're growing fast, the business will consume every dollar it makes and then some to fuel that growth. You might be showing solid profits on the income statement, but that cash is likely tied up in inventory, receivables, new hires, equipment, or facility upgrades. Growth reinvests your profits for you, whether you like it or not.

If you want to actually *peel off cash* for yourself or your partners, you need to slow down growth, at least temporarily. Once you stop feeding the beast (no new fixed assets, no working capital expansion), that cash starts accumulating in the bank.

Now, your business is throwing off real, distributable cash, not just paper profits.

Get Brad's free Cash Flow Planning template (Excel) and start washing away your cash flow issues (https://bradpoulos.com/business-resources#CashFlowPlanning).

Original post URL: https://bradpoulos.com/cash-flow-issues/

Contractor vs Employee

Originally posted on July 1, 2025.

Getting It Right in the Eyes of the CRA (and Your Wallet)

When I was still in the corporate world, my employer had a number of individuals that we determined were "contractors." It was a mutually beneficial arrangement between the two parties.

The company liked it because it saves some payroll taxes (including WSIB, which can be expensive), but perhaps more importantly, it brings flexibility. The company could modulate the workforce to match the workload. In a project-oriented business like ours that was an important benefit.

The contractors liked it because they earned a higher wage and enjoyed additional autonomy. They could also incorporate if desired, claiming more deductions and lowering taxes. The downside for them was that they didn't have the protections that being an employee brings under the law.

This means no notice or severance pay, no Employment Insurance, and no paid time off for vacation, family matters, or illness.

It also means no benefits, such as pension, health, or dental coverage, and no Workers' Compensation, which can be important in some jobs.

The Consequences of Getting It Wrong

CRA audited us and found that they were contractors in name only and declared these folks employees. It cost us well into the six figures for back CPP and EI contributions (interestingly, the "employees" had no liability).

Understanding the difference between a contractor and an employee is critical for small business owners. Whether you're growing your team or outsourcing your next project, this decision can carry financial and legal consequences.

Let's unpack what you need to know to make the right call.

The CRA's Perspective: Intent and Facts

The CRA doesn't care what you call someone on paper. You can have a beautifully worded agreement that calls someone an independent contractor, but if their role looks, smells, and functions like employment, the CRA will treat them like an employee.

The Canada Revenue Agency uses a two-part test: intent and facts. First, they'll consider the intention of both parties at the time of engagement. But far more important is the second part, which examines how the relationship actually operates day to day.

The core factors the CRA uses include control (who decides how and when the work gets done), ownership of tools, chance of profit or risk of loss, and integration into the business. If the worker is dependent on you, works only for you, uses your tools, and is tightly supervised then they're probably an employee.

Here are some of the key questions that CRA considers:

- Can the worker control the method of doing the work?
- Does the worker have the power to control and discipline other employees?
- Can the worker hire and fire other employees?
- Where does the worker get most of their income from?
- Does the worker work exclusively (or almost exclusively) for the employer?
- Can the worker determine the place of work?
- Does the worker have much freedom in performing the work?
- Is the worker supervised?
- Does the worker have the power to delegate?
- Can the worker prescribe exactly the work to be done?
- Does the worker use their own tools?
- Does the worker have a risk of losing their own money?
- Does the worker do the same thing as employees?

Pros and Cons: Contractors vs Employees

Hiring a contractor often feels simpler.

No payroll, no deductions, no long-term commitment.

But that simplicity can come with risk.

Here's how the trade-offs typically stack up:

Aspect	Contractor	Employee
Flexibility	High – can easily end contract	Low – ESA rules apply
Cost	Lower (no CPP, EI, benefits)	Higher all-in cost
Control	Lower – can't dictate how/when	Higher – you set hours/methods
Risk of Penalties	High if misclassified	Low
Commitment/ Buy-in	Often lower	Typically higher

Cost Comparison: The Real Price Tag

Let's take a $50/hour worker as an example. If you hire them as a contractor, you pay $50 an hour. That's it. No deductions, no admin, no vacation or holiday pay.

But if they're an employee, your true cost might look more like $60–$65 an hour once you account for employer contributions to CPP and EI, paid vacation, statutory holidays, and the time spent on payroll and paperwork.

Additionally, employees enjoy further privileges under the Employment Standards Act, including specific notice periods and termination rules.

The Penalty for Getting It Wrong

As the opening story illustrates, misclassifying a worker can come back to haunt you. If the CRA or a provincial authority finds that your contractor is actually an employee, you could be on the hook for retroactive CPP and EI contributions, interest, penalties, and even unpaid vacation or overtime. WSIB, too, if they get wind of it.

This isn't theoretical.

In high-profile cases like the famous Foodora case, Canadian courts ruled that gig workers were actually dependent contractors, entitled to many of the same protections as employees.

How to Stay on the Right Side of the CRA

The safest way to avoid misclassification is to structure the relationship correctly from the start. A few tips:

- Focus on actual working conditions, not just contract language.
- Check out the CRA's RC4110 guide to review classification (https://www.canada.ca/en/revenue-agency/services/forms-publications/publications/rc4110/employee-self-employed.html)
- Get a formal ruling from the CRA if you're unsure: https://www.canada.ca/en/revenue-agency/services/forms-publications/publications/rc4110/employee-self-employed.html#toc4

When to Use Each

Contractors are best when the work is project-based, the person brings their own tools or expertise, and they clearly work with multiple clients. Employees are a better choice when the work is core to your business, you want control over the output, or you're looking for long-term continuity.

This Isn't Just a Tax Question

It's a strategic business decision. Hiring contractors might save you money upfront, but the trade-off is less control and potentially more risk. Hiring employees costs more, but can provide stability and commitment.

The key is to be deliberate. If you treat a contractor like an employee, don't be surprised when the CRA agrees with you.

Original post URL: https://bradpoulos.com/contractor-vs-employee/

Why I Swear by Paralegals (and You Should Too)

Originally posted on June 16, 2025.

How a $35K courtroom loss taught me the value of affordable legal firepower

When Legal Help Isn't Optional

Legal issues show up in small business more often than most owners expect. Eventually you're going to need help with the nuances of contracts, dismissals, late payments, or disputes over deliverables. And while most people default to calling a lawyer, the smart operator knows there's a more cost-effective alternative to a full-scope lawyer.

The trick is knowing when you need a $500/hour litigator, and when a qualified paralegal can do the job just as well (or better).

Paralegals vs. Lawyers: What's the Difference?

Once seen as junior assistants to lawyers, paralegals today operate in a much more independent role. In many jurisdictions, including Ontario where I live, they can:

- provide legal advice within specific areas;
- represent clients in Small Claims Court, traffic matters, and certain tribunals;
- draft and review legal documents;
- handle landlord-tenant disputes, employment standards issues;
- serve as a notary public; and,
- much more.

They are prohibited from the following activities:

- representing you in criminal matters, family law matters, or higher courts;
- drafting or reviewing wills or handling real estate transactions.

Note: As of mid-2025, Ontario will begin licensing Family Legal Services

Provider (FLSP) paralegals for limited family law representation (mainly uncontested separations and support filings), but full family-law work remains lawyer-only.

For current details on paralegal scope of practice in Ontario, visit: https://lso.ca/public-resources/legal-service-options/paralegals/about-paralegals

Why Most Small Biz Legal Work Doesn't Need a Lawyer

Most of the legal challenges a small business faces fall well within a paralegal's domain:

- Employee terminations and wrongful dismissal claims (in Small Claims)
- Debt collection under $35,000
- Contractor disputes
- Landlord/tenant and lease issues
- Civil matters heard by administrative tribunals
- Reviewing contracts
- Drafting basic employment contracts (in permitted cases)

When it comes to everyday operational legal support, paralegals can be not just sufficient, but ideal. And the kicker? Their hourly rate is often half (or less) of what a lawyer would charge.

Lessons from the Most Humbling Courtroom Moment of My Career

Years ago, I stepped in to run a metalworking company while the owner took time off. Before I showed up, the sales manager had been fired with cause. The paperwork was pristine. The file had been managed by the owner's friend who was a labour negotiator for one of Canada's largest companies, and was the best documented "firing file" I have ever seen. The sales manager had been placed on a formal Performance Improvement Plan. Multiple written warnings followed. A textbook termination. So when she later sued the company for wrongful dismissal in Small Claims Court, we figured we were golden. The owner and I, both confident and armed with the cleanest HR file I'd ever seen, decided to handle the defence ourselves. The plaintiff showed up with a paralegal.

And that paralegal absolutely *demolished* our case. He eviscerated the owner on cross-examination. The judge, in her ruling, said she regretted that the Small Claims Court limited her award to $35,000, because our side had caused the plaintiff "significant harm." It was a humbling, expensive, and unforgettable lesson.

From that point forward, I've used paralegals regularly, and with excellent results.

The Smart Operator's Strategy: Build a Paralegal Relationship

Don't wait for a crisis to start looking for help. Build a relationship now with a reputable paralegal and use them proactively. Have them review your standard contracts and get their advice on employee terminations before they become legal problems.

Let them handle demand letters and collections so you're not chasing money on your own. You'll not only save money. You'll get practical, responsive help from someone who understands your business.

Quick Checklist: When a Paralegal Can Probably Handle It

- Small claims under $35K
- Lease disputes and evictions
- Contract disputes with customers or contractors
- Unpaid invoices and collections
- Tribunal hearings (e.g., WSIB, landlord-tenant, employment standards)
- Employee terminations (where Small Claims Court applies)
- Assist with drafting straightforward employment agreements and reviewing standard contracts.

Final Word: Saving Money Isn't About Cheap—It's About Fit

You don't need to lawyer up for every issue. You just need the *right* help for the job. Paralegals aren't second-class legal citizens; they're just first-class value.

Smart business isn't about spending less. It's about getting the most value for what you do spend.

That's why I keep a paralegal in my contacts.

And why you should too.

Original post URL: https://bradpoulos.com/paralegals/

Getting Paid Faster Without Begging

Originally posted on June 9, 2025.

Techniques to Improve A/R Turnover Without Discounting

It's often said that if your customer owes you $1,000, they have a problem. But if they owe you $1 million, then it's your problem. Nothing could be more true.

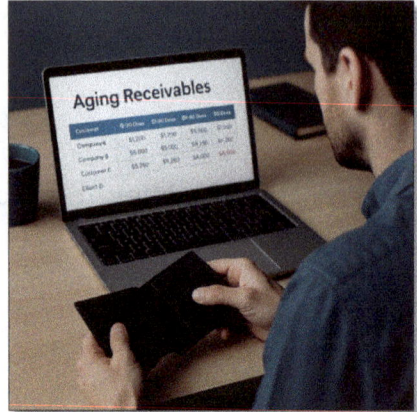

During the heyday of the dot-com boom, a slew of wireless operators emerged offering services in high-frequency bands called LMDS and MMDS. One such company, Maxlink, was using LMDS to provide commercial data service in Canada.

The day they went bankrupt, they owed us nothing. But just one month prior, they owed us over $1 million. That amount of bad debt would have spelled bankruptcy for our small company, which had only $11.5 million in sales that year.

I had allowed the allure of large orders to overtake my judgment. I knew these technologies weren't viable. I had said so myself, but we still chased the orders. Worse, we extended them credit terms we couldn't really afford and they weren't worthy of. That experience taught me the value of trusting my gut when assessing credit risk.

Managing accounts receivable is crucial to your business health, cash flow, and working capital efficiency. There are ways of getting paid faster that don't carry the high costs of early-payment discounts, factoring and the like.

Know Where You Stand

Start by running an accounts receivable aging report.

This report will show you exactly who owes you money and how long their invoices have been outstanding. In a smaller business, reviewing this on a weekly basis might be sufficient.

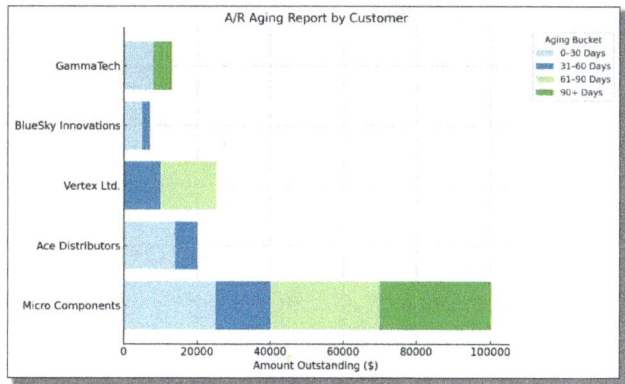

A/R Aging Report by Customer

However, once your operation reaches a certain size, it becomes crucial to have someone on your team reviewing it daily.

From there, calculate your "Days Receivable" using the formula:

$$Days\ Receivable = \frac{Average\ Accounts\ Receivable}{Average\ Daily\ Credit\ Sales}$$

This simple ratio provides a snapshot of how efficiently your company converts sales into actual cash in the bank. Now, benchmark yourself against the average in your industry and ask how you're doing.

It can really vary based on what kind of business you're in. If your customers are general retailers, you're likely getting paid in 30 – 45 days. Manufacturing and tech are closer to 45 or 60, and industries like construction, mining, or other resource extraction run 90+ days. At the other end of the spectrum, restaurants can be lucky if their suppliers give them 7 or 14 days to pay!

If you're unsure about your industry, visit this page at ReadyRatios.com for guidance.

If you're nailing your collections and are getting paid faster than your peers, kudos to you. And if your Days Receivable significantly exceeds that industry benchmark, and you're plagued with cash flow issues, then it's time to rethink your credit policies. First, segment your customers:

- Habitual late payers
- Slow but reliable
- Fast payers

Be careful here. Credit management is part art, part science, and this story from my book is a great example of how 'one size does not fit all.'

Susanna and Alex

Susanna, our new credit manager, flagged a $100K+ outstanding balance from Micro Components Ltd. They were a long-standing customer who bought both large and small-ticket items. While they always paid late, they also always paid in full. Their owner Alex was a very ethical and serious engineer who prided himself on his professional reputation. He had A+ customers despite only being about a $10 million company. Susanna didn't know their history or that their customers were the U.S. and Canadian military, who are notoriously slow payers.

She wanted to cut off Micro Components but I explained how they were a very loyal customer who had never failed to pay - they had just also never failed to pay late. Susanna was rightfully concerned not knowing the history, and further was concerned because her bonus was based on days receivable across the board. To solve that we adjusted how we calculated aging and kept shipping to Alex. That's why rigid rules don't work when managing credit.

Fix What's Broken in Your Process

Start by invoicing immediately and making those invoices crystal clear. Vague descriptions or missing purchase order numbers are a gift to slow-paying customers, offering them a built-in excuse to delay payment. Eliminate those excuses from the outset.

Next, use invoicing tools that support automatic reminders. Most modern accounting systems and small business ERPs have this feature built in, and it saves both time and awkward follow-ups.

You should also make it as easy as possible for customers to pay. Accept multiple payment methods—credit card, ACH, e-transfer, payment links, even QR codes. The fewer clicks it takes to pay you, the better.

Finally, be realistic when setting payment terms. Look at your industry norms and respect them. You can't push a rope uphill, and if you try to force unusually tight terms on your customers, you might just push them away entirely.

Train Your Customers and You'll Be Getting Paid Faster!

It pays, literally, to be proactive. A day or two before an invoice is due, pick up the phone and make a courtesy call. Something along the lines of, "Just checking that we're in the queue for payment," is enough. It's a gentle nudge that keeps you top of mind without sounding confrontational and reminds your customers that you're a stickler for payment.

For brand-new customers, use signaling theory to communicate how you expect to be treated. By following up diligently on your first few invoices, you're training your customer that you don't let payments slip through the cracks, and that if they do, they can count on hearing from that pest Brad.

Sometimes, especially with larger invoices, it helps if the owner personally gets involved. When a customer delayed payment, I used to say, "You know Bill, when I took your order, I was really excited about being your supplier. But I didn't think I was signing up to be your bank."

You're not being rude. You're running a business.

If payment doesn't come after the initial follow-up, escalate the tone and frequency. A professional collections process might look like this: a friendly reminder, followed by a second notice, and then a final notice indicating possible credit hold or legal action. You're going to alternate between phone and email based on the circumstances.

A Note About Late Fees

Late fees are often a point of confusion in business transactions. Many companies put them on their invoices, but unless those fees were clearly agreed to in advance, ideally as part of a signed contract, they're usually meaningless. Most commercial buyers treat these line items as suggestions rather than obligations. In over two decades of running businesses, I've probably seen late fees listed on hundreds of supplier invoices and statements. And not once have I paid a dime in late fees unless I was contractually bound to do so.

The distinction here is important. With a credit card, for example, you agree in writing to a schedule of fees and penalties. If you pay late, you've accepted that interest will accrue and that the credit issuer has the legal right to enforce it. However, when a vendor simply adds a "2% per month late fee" line to your invoice without any underlying agreement, it's rarely enforceable. Unless both parties have explicitly agreed to those terms in advance, either by contract or through detailed purchase order (PO) terms, most customers will likely ignore them. I suggest you do the same.

Rethink Customer Risk

Credit decisions aren't just binary—it's not always a simple "yes" or "no." Sometimes the most strategic answer is "yes, and..." meaning, yes, we'll extend you credit, and here's how we're going to do it.

One of the most effective ways to manage risk is through milestone billing or requiring partial prepayments. These techniques are particularly valuable in service-based businesses or custom manufacturing, where upfront costs are substantial and timelines are long. Breaking payments into chunks tied to deliverables keeps everyone aligned and protects your cash flow.

For clients who have slipped into late payment habits but still want to place orders, consider shifting them to a "COD+" arrangement. This means cash on delivery, plus a small additional amount that chips away at their outstanding balance. It's a fair, enforceable compromise that keeps business moving without deepening your risk.

For larger orders or when dealing with brand-new clients, it's smart to run a credit check using services like Dun & Bradstreet or Equifax. If something seems off—or if your gut just doesn't sit right—ask for a deposit. You'll be surprised how often this request is met with immediate compliance. Responsible companies usually don't balk at basic risk management.

If you're unsure where to start or want to formalize this process, I've created a simple downloadable checklist to guide your new-customer assessments. You can grab it here: https://bradpoulos.com/wp-content/uploads/2025/05/New-Customer-Credit-Checklist.pdf

Getting paid faster means setting expectations, removing friction, and standing your ground.

Original post URL: https://bradpoulos.com/getting-paid-faster-without-begging/

SALES AND MARKETING

Tell Me Right Now—Why Can't We Raise Your Prices?)

Originally posted on September 6, 2025.

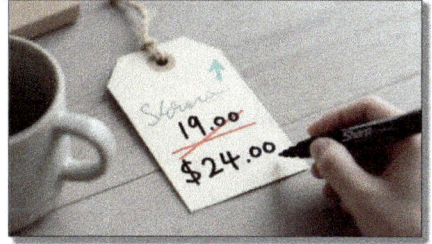

Part of my schtick is that when first meeting a new client, I will almost always ask:

"Tell me right now, why can't we raise your prices?"

It might sound blunt, but it cuts straight to one of the most underused levers in small business: pricing. Raising your prices is the fastest, cleanest way to boost profit. No new hires. No marketing spend. No equipment upgrades. Just new bottom-line dollars.

But I will lose some customers!

Maybe. Customers always come and go. And if you raise your prices, there's no doubt that you will, at the margin, have a few drop off. The good news is that it's likely the most price-sensitive ones, who are often a pain in the ass, and should have a PITA premium applied anyway (see the article called *Firing Customers. Letting the Bottom 10% Go...*) for an explanation.

The heart of this tactic is understanding the trade-off between volume and margin. Let's say your business has an average gross profit margin of 40%. If you raise your prices by 5%, how many customers can you afford to lose without this resulting in a net margin loss?

Here's the formula for you to try:

$$Allowable\ Drop\ in\ Volume = \frac{Price\ Increase}{Price\ Increase\ +\ Profit\ Margin}$$

[everything is in %]

So in our case, the allowable drop in volume before we lose $ of margin is:

$$Allowable\ Drop\ in\ Volume = \frac{5\%}{5\% + 40\%} = \frac{.05}{.45} = 11.1\%$$

We can raise prices by 5%, and if we don't lose any more than 11% of (arguably our worst) customers, we will be ahead, dollar-wise.

Overcoming Your Emotional Resistance

Many business owners flinch at this idea. They hesitate; not because the numbers don't work, but because fear, uncertainty and doubt kick in. Fear of losing customers. Or seeming greedy. Uncertainty about what you'll do if too many walk. And doubt that you're not actually worth it.

Fear not! Your customers likely aren't as price-sensitive as you think. An interesting study from Boston Consulting Group indicates that while people say price matters, it rarely drives the final decision, and when it is a factor, it will depend on the market, category, or buying situation. You may not skimp on date night with your sweetheart, but you are budget-conscious when out with the kids for dinner.

There's some solid academic theory, but it's backed up by experience. In an earlier article (*Customer Warning Signs: How to Spot Trouble Before It Hits Your Business*), I outlined how I increased prices to Nortel, and they never even flinched. Our sales department was worried that we'd lose business, but we never lost a single deal on price.

Price As A Signal of Value

This Price-Quality heuristic has been confirmed across multiple industries. In fact, a higher price can *increase* perceived value, sometimes dramatically. There is a lot of research on this. Mats Godenhielm states in his study "High Price Signals High Quality" argues that "sellers cannot credibly communicate the quality they offer, and consequently price acts as a signal of quality."

We assume expensive things are better.

My dad was given the task of running Junior Achievement's Canadian Business Hall of Fame dinner in the late 1970s or early 1980s. The attendance had been dropping off, and they were no longer attracting the elite of Toronto's business crowd to the event.

One of the tactics he used was to more than double the price of a table from $500 to $1,250. I remember my dad saying, "the CEO of [a big 5] bank doesn't want to go to a $50 a plate dinner!"

They sold out for the next several years in a row.

That was a very early lesson for me on the power of price not only as a driver of profit, but as a differentiator. Look at how companies like Starbucks, Apple, and every high-end fashion house or luxury accessories brand command above-average prices.

Communicating Your Value

If a customer pushes back on price, it might not mean you're too expensive. It might mean you haven't clearly communicated why you're worth what you charge.

Your job is to make the value so clear that the price feels like a bargain.

A few years ago, I was coaching the salesperson at a metalworking company. He was lamenting that the customers were saying we were expensive. My answer was that next time it happened, I wanted him to respond, "I know," and then explain that our products are of higher quality than the competition, and we provide better service, which isn't free. I said he should acknowledge, but never apologize.

Your price tells a story. It signals your place in the market. Low prices may attract bargain hunters but repel the customers you actually want who are willing to pay for quality, reliability, or alignment with their values.

You don't have to overhaul your pricing overnight. Start small.

Test new prices on new customers.

Even better, consider adding a premium version of your existing offering or rolling out a tiered pricing model.

Giving customers multiple choices accommodates different budgets, and if done well, can use price as a signal to steer customers to your most profitable tier, while making the customer feel that the chosen product was a smart, high-value choice.

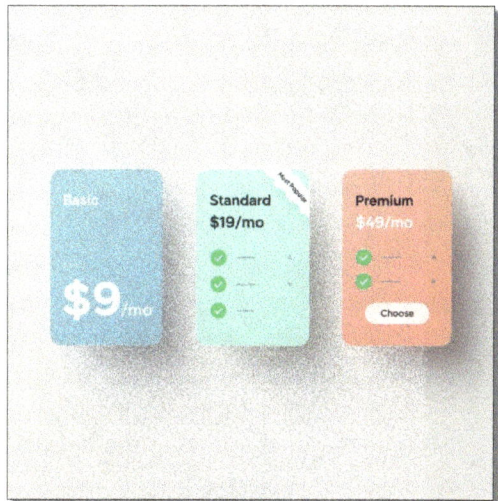

As always, data is your friend.

Measure everything and adjust as needed.

But before you chase new revenue streams or crank up marketing spend, ask yourself:

Why can't we raise our prices?

You may not have a good answer.

Original post URL: https://bradpoulos.com/small-business-pricing

In B2B, Who'll Really Close the Sale? (Hint: Not Who You Think)

Originally posted on May 21, 2025.

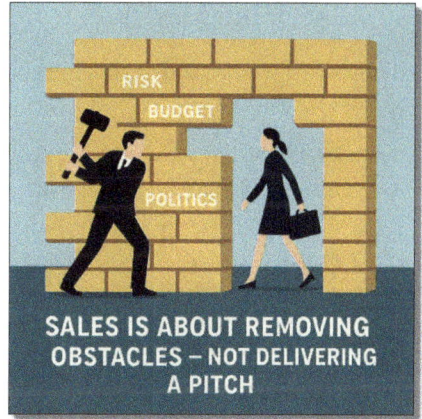

SALES IS ABOUT REMOVING OBSTACLES – NOT DELIVERING A PITCH

> *"The smartest thing a salesperson can do? Know when to shut up and let the customer close themselves."*
> *- Dan Pink (author of To Sell is Human)*

If you spend any time around sales trainers or sales books you'll hear the phrase "close the sale" used like a magic trick. A job left to the masters who have honed their craft to a fine edge through decades of hard slugging in the sales trenches.

> *"You've got to close the deal!"*
> *"Here are 17 closing techniques that work every time!"*

Back in the day, we'd sometimes bring in the VP or even the company President to seal a deal and "close the sale" with a big customer. I once sat in on a meeting where we flew in the Senior VP of Sales from Hughes Network Systems to help us land a major Canadian client (our telecom services were based on Hughes' hardware products). He was polished. And I was impressed with his poise and mastery of the spoken word, but here's what I didn't realize at the time:

He wasn't really closing.

Because in complex B2B sales, the customer closes the deal, not you.

The salesperson's job isn't to "close."

That's almost icky. This approach reminds one of the back-slapping, hard-drinking and off-colour joke-telling stereotype made famous by Herb Tarlek of Cincinnati WKRP fame, or worse, Alec Baldwin's unforgettable Blake in that black comedy sales masterpiece, Glengarry Glenross.

Those position the sales field as one of manipulation and zero-sum games, neither of which has to be true.

That's not what good B2B selling looks like.

The salesperson's real job?

To remove the barriers to closure, and then — when the time is right — have the discipline to say no.

Let me explain.

Part 1: You Don't Close the Sale - Customers Close Themselves

Salespeople don't make customers buy.

Customers decide to buy when they've resolved enough of their internal resistance to act, and when their fear, uncertainty, and doubt have been diminished enough that any perceived risk of buying from you is outweighed by the anticipated benefits of your product or service.

That resistance might look like:

BARRIERS TO CLOSING THE SALE

- UNCERTAINTY ABOUT ROI
- INTERNAL POLITICS
- BUDGET CONCERNS
- RISK AVERSION
- INERTIA

- Technical concerns
- Political risk in switching suppliers
- Budget anxiety
- Or just inertia — especially if they're working with an industry giant (you know, the "no one ever got fired for buying IBM" effect).

Your job isn't to push. It's to peel those layers back and remove friction. You're not a magician. You're a barrier remover.

You:

- eliminate technical confusion;
- craft the right offer for the customer's situation;
- navigate internal politics, both in the customer and in your own firm;
- manage timing and expectations;

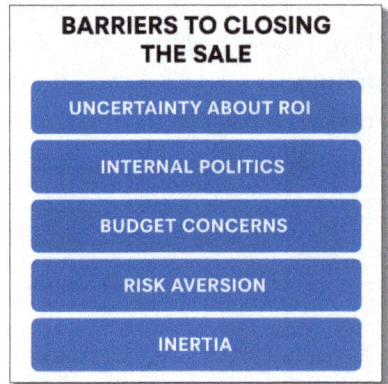

- prove value;
- advocate for the customer;
- and yes, get the pricing right.

When the deal is right for them, the customer will move forward.

A true "closer" creates the conditions where saying yes feels obvious.

Part 2: The Customers Closes When You Finally Say "No"

Here's the counterintuitive piece that trips up even seasoned sellers:

The sale doesn't close when the customer says "yes."

It closes when the salesperson finally says "no."

In long-cycle industrial B2B sales, the customer will keep asking until you stop giving.

You show your pricing. They push back. You go against your better judgment and give a small discount.

They ask for extended payment terms. Yours are usually 45 days, and your credit department is pretty strict. But it's a huge sale, and you escalate to the senior management and negotiate that you can give them 60 days.

They want extra site visits, or a custom demo, or a slightly different scope, so you deliver.

How about some free training? Sure. Why not!?

Or throwing in a year's (or two's) maintenance fees.

Customers are like any other person or entity. And you are training them to believe that asking equals receiving.

So they keep asking.

They're not being jerks. They're smart buyers doing their job: extracting every drop of value before they commit.

And they'll keep doing it until you draw the line.

The sale only closes when the salesperson finally says "No."

That's when the customer realizes:

- They've gotten everything they're going to get
- The terms are clear
- It's time to decide

If you've done the job right and built value, resolved doubts, and stayed aligned, they'll close. But they won't close while they think there's still juice to squeeze.

Train Them How To Treat You

Every sales interaction sets a precedent.

- Say yes too often → they expect more "yeses"
- Fold under pressure → they keep applying it
- Act like you need the deal → they treat it like charity

But if you demonstrate value, hold your ground, and remain professionally firm, they'll respect you.

And that'll close the sale.

Saying "no" is how you teach the customer it's time to decide.

How I Learned to say No

I was Director of Sales and Marketing for a telecom services company. We only made a few (very large) sales each year. Our average deal was multiple six-figures and our clients were large companies, governments and other global telecom carriers.

We had one buyer, Jim, who worked for a large Canadian retailer that must remain nameless, but was incorporated in the 17th century. Jim was the most frustrating customer. He dragged things out for around nine months. Every time we thought we were close, he'd come back with something:

- A revised quote with slightly altered spec requests
- Extended terms of 75 days when our standard was 30
- On-site demo

- Revisions to our standard contract
- A longer warranty

My salesperson, Arsh, kept saying yes — trying to be helpful, trying to keep the deal alive.

But the deal didn't move. It just lingered.

Eventually, our Sales Manager, Shannon, Arsh's boss, stepped in. She had Arsh set up a meeting with Jim.

Shannon didn't do a pitch. She said:

"Jim, we've made every accommodation we can. Arsh has put forward our best offer in terms of scope, pricing, and terms. If it works, we're ready to start putting dishes on rooves but if not, no hard feelings. We'll move on."

Jim signed the PO and faxed it the next day. (It was 2005, after all.)

He didn't need another concession. He wasn't waiting to be convinced.

He needed clarity.

Once we drew the line, he made the decision.

That's how real B2B sales close. Not with a slick pitch, but with a confident no at the right time.

Close the Sale? Nope!

In complex B2B sales:

- You don't close the customer. You help them close themselves.
- You do that by removing friction, building value, and then, when it counts, saying no.

That final "no" creates a boundary. And boundaries create clarity.

And clarity leads to decisions.

Original post URL: https://bradpoulos.com/close-the-sale/

We've Been Teaching Our Kids Break Even All Wrong

Originally posted on May 26, 2025.

Many of the best tools in business are quite simple in their concept and application. The break-even point, or break even analysis, is a helpful signal that takes little effort to calculate and monitor.

Despite that simplicity, many practitioners overlook it.

Others misunderstand it, often because of the way it is presented in business school textbooks. Or they misuse it, not understanding the difference between fixed and variable costs, or how to separate them in the analysis.

Before we go on, a few definitions:

Fixed Costs: expenses that remain constant regardless of the quantity of goods produced or services provided by a business. These costs are also known as overhead or indirect costs and are not directly tied to production levels. Think things like rent, insurance, and utilities.

Variable costs: are business expenses that fluctuate directly with the volume of goods produced or services provided. When production or sales increase, variable costs also increase, and when production or sales decrease, variable costs decrease. Examples include raw materials, direct labour, and packaging materials.

Unit Contribution Margin: This is the amount of the sales revenue that remains after paying the variable costs. Think of it as the profit on a single unit of sales.

Contribution Margin Ratio: This is the contribution margin expressed as a percentage of the selling price.

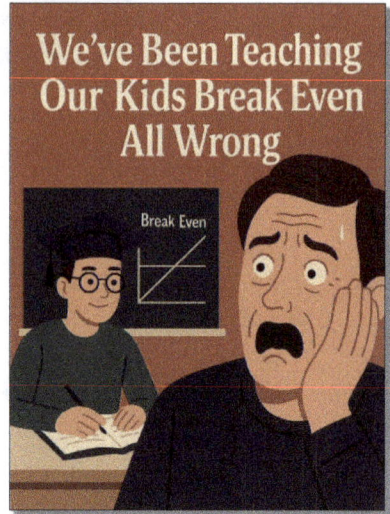

Why the Traditional Break Even Model Falls Apart

Do a web search on the term "break-even point" or browse any business school's first-year textbook and you'll see that they almost universally present a graph that looks like this:

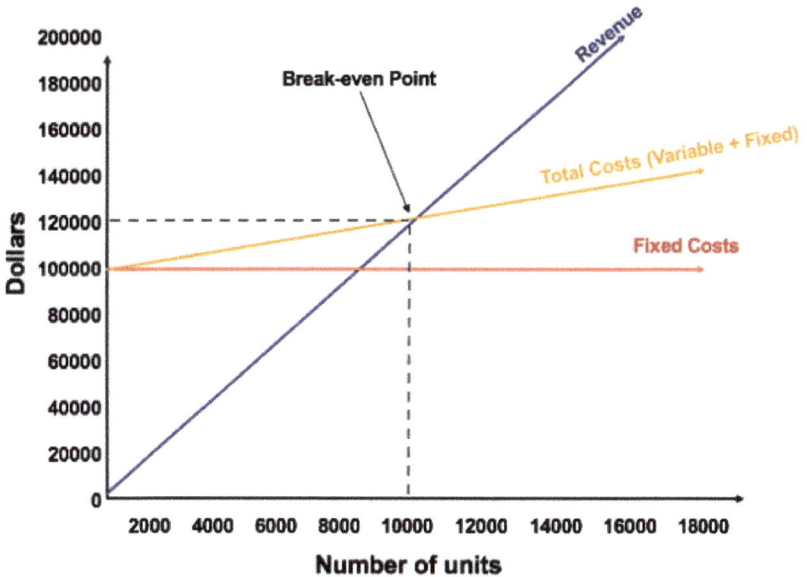

For a given period of time the fixed costs are determined. Then the Total Costs are identified by adding the variable costs (yellow line).

A separate (blue) line shows how total revenues grow with volume. The point where they cross is where you are moving from a cumulative loss position (not having yet covered your total costs) to where each sale now adds to your cumulative profits.

And note that the answer comes out in units. You'll find the formula for all of this:

$$Break\ Even\ (units) = \frac{Fixed\ Costs}{Unit\ Contribution\ Margin}$$ It's not untrue. It's

great on paper.

From a teaching point of view, it's even somewhat useful for demonstrating the *concept*, but here's the thing...

What number will you use for Unit Contribution Margin? Remember, that's the $ profit on one unit.

One unit of what?!

No real-world business sells just one product at one price with one tidy margin.

If you're like 99% of businesses, you've got a range of products and services that have different levels of margins and sell at different prices. What is the unit contribution margin for a restaurant?

They sell a soda pop for $3.99, with a contribution margin of approximately 98%, and a $79 steak with a 60% contribution margin. Which one would you use?

The textbook approach to break-even point analysis is not possible with this data set, but there is an approach that can be useful to the small business owner, and on a daily basis.

Ditch the unit count. Track break even in dollars.

Most companies have an overall average margin that they're trying to achieve. This is driven largely by one's industry and the forces at play at any time. An average fast casual restaurant might be aiming for a 65% contribution margin ratio, while some retailers settle for 30%. Some distributors work on single-digit margins!

So, rather than calculating some theoretical unit break even volume figure for your company, we use the same formula but instead make the answer come out in TOTAL $ sales.

Then, turn that into a daily sales target. And monitor it every day!

It's way more useful, more manageable, and — importantly — more actionable.

There are just three numbers that every owner needs to make that daily check-in real. To calculate the break-even sales figure you need to know your monthly fixed costs and your average contribution margin ratio.

Then just compare that to the third number, which is your sales on any given day.

If you're unsure of your industry's average contribution margin ratio, you should be able to easily find it through a web search. Fullratio.com published a list of industries with average gross profit margins (a very close proxy to contribution margin).

A More Useful Break Even Formula

This formula will determine what dollar volume of revenue you need to break even, given your fixed costs, and an estimate of your percentage of contribution margin.

$$Break\ Even\ [\$] = \frac{Fixed\ Costs}{Contribution\ Margin\ [in\ \%]}$$

Assume a small wholesale business with the following costs:

- Monthly Fixed Costs = $10,500
- Average Contribution Margin = 35%

$$Break\ Even\ [\$] = \frac{10,500}{0.35} = \$30,000$$

But they are only open 21 days per month on average. Their daily break-even point is:

$$Daily\ Break\ Even\ [\$] = \frac{Daily\ Fixed\ Costs}{Contribution\ Margin\ [in\ \%]} \text{ .so...}$$

$$Daily\ Break\ Even\ [\$] = \frac{10,500 \div 21}{0.35} = \frac{500}{0.35} = \$1,429$$

If you don't sell at least $1,429 each day they are open, they're not covering their overhead costs.

The 5 PM Gut Check: A Real-World Habit

Back when I was running a bricks-and-mortar operation, I had a ritual. At the end of each day, usually around 5 p.m., I'd ask my controller or one of the accounting people one simple question:

"What were sales today?"

If they gave me a number above our daily break-even, I'd drive home relaxed and somewhat satisfied. If the number was below our daily break even, or hovering near the edge, on any kind of semi-regular basis then I'd start turning over rocks:

- Is traffic down?
- Are we discounting too much?
- Is our labour cost out of line?
- Do we have the wrong product mix?

That one daily pulse check kept me grounded. I didn't need a P&L every week. I already knew.

What This Approach Gives You

- **Real-time clarity**: You'll know, daily, if things are going well.
- **Smarter decisions**: About pricing, staffing, promotions, and purchasing.
- **Less stress**: You're not wondering how you're doing. You'll know.
- **Better use of your energy**: You'll focus on the right levers.

Bottom Line

If you're running a small business, forget the five-tab spreadsheet.

You need three numbers, one formula, and the discipline to check in daily.

Because if you don't know whether you made money today... You probably didn't.

Original post URL: https://bradpoulos.com/break-even/

Firing Customers. Letting the Bottom 10% Go...

Originally posted on June 6, 2025.

Most small business owners hang onto every customer like their life depends on it.

It doesn't. You need to start firing customers.

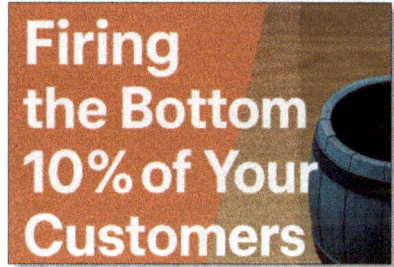

Your loyalty to the bottom 10% of customers — the ones who drain your time, your team, and your margins — is costing you more than you may realize.

Let's talk about how to spot them, what they're really costing you, and why letting them go might be the most profitable decision you make this year.

Not All Revenue Is Good Revenue

We've been taught that more customers = good business. But that's not universally true. There are two kinds of revenue: profitable and unprofitable.

Your worst customers occupy the latter category and will undoubtedly:

- Argue about pricing or nickel-and-dime you;
- Take twice as long to serve as everyone else;
- Disrespect your boundaries or your team;
- Pay late or screw with your cash flow;
- Derail your focus with custom requests that don't scale.

The Real Cost of Serving Your Bottom 10%

These customers:

- Distract you from your best clients;
- Burn out your team;
- Break your processes with constant exceptions;
- Drain your energy and derail your strategy.

All of which have costs.

Consider Client A who pays $1,500/month and takes 12 hours to service.

Another Client B pays $1,200/month and takes 3 hours.

Who's actually more profitable? Which kind do you want to scale up and which do you want to wean yourself from?

Identifying the Bottom 10% doesn't need to be complicated. It's often pretty intuitive.

Ask yourself:

- Who do I dread hearing from?
- Who always needs "just one more thing"?
- Who pays the least but demands the most?
- Who's outside my ideal client profile?
- Who would I not take on today?

This isn't about personality. It's about fit, friction, and focus.

Getting Precise: Use Activity-Based Costing

To go beyond gut feel, use activity-based costing (ABC) in your accounting. ABC tracks actual revenues earned and resources used — like service hours, admin support, or endless follow-ups — and ties them to each client.

It forces you to assign costs based on where the firm is expending resources. It's a more accurate approach than traditional costing, especially in service businesses.

Allocating Overhead Fairly

Some of your costs can't be attributed to a particular customer or project. Think about the infrastructure it takes to stay open for business — rent, software, insurance, admin salaries, even the breakroom coffee. These costs aren't tied to specific clients but still have to be covered.

To fully cost a particular customer or project, we add an assigned amount of overhead to their other costs. To assign overhead fairly, pick what you think is the most appropriate in your instance from these two most common, practical options:

Flat % of revenue – Easy, but simplistic.

Hours-based – More hours = more overhead. Probably better in a service business.

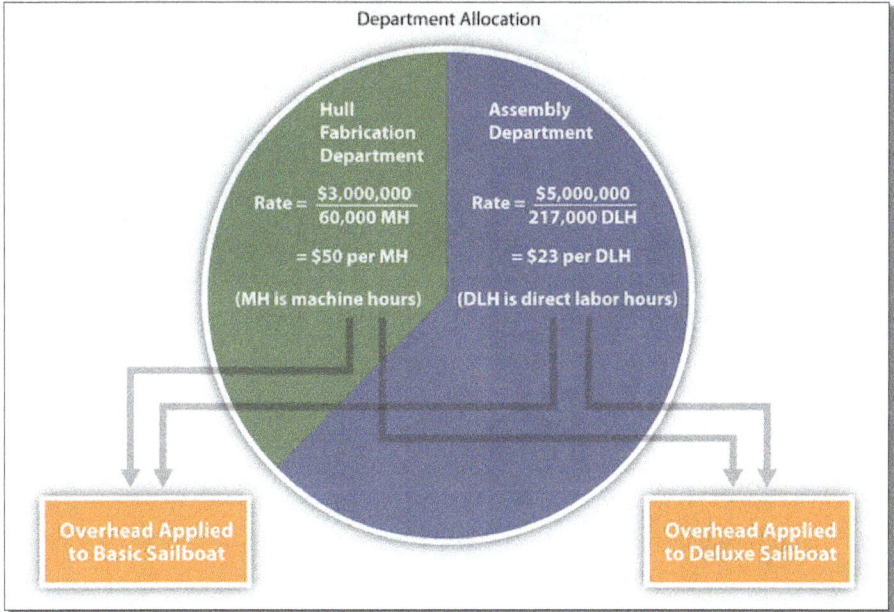

Department Allocation

Hull Fabrication Department

$$\text{Rate} = \frac{\$3,000,000}{60,000 \text{ MH}}$$

$$= \$50 \text{ per MH}$$

(MH is machine hours)

Assembly Department

$$\text{Rate} = \frac{\$5,000,000}{217,000 \text{ DLH}}$$

$$= \$23 \text{ per DLH}$$

(DLH is direct labor hours)

Overhead Applied to Basic Sailboat

Overhead Applied to Deluxe Sailboat

The goal isn't perfection. It's reasonableness. You know your business. Use a method you can repeat, compare, and make decisions from.

Letting Go Makes Room for Better Business

Some argue that if a customer covers their variable costs, like materials, direct labour, or delivery expenses and contributes anything to overhead, they're worth keeping. That's fine if they're easy to work with.

But if they're needy, disorganized, or toxic, that thin contribution isn't worth the drag. That mindset traps you in scarcity mode, like clinging to a leaky boat, assuming you can't replace them.

The truth? You usually can.

You just need the courage to replace them with a better-fit customer, one who brings higher margins without the chaos.

When you trim your bottom 10%, you free up time, energy, and resources to serve your best customers better, or welcome new ones who fit.

The Head Fake: You're Not Really Firing Customers

Here's the head fake, a nod to Randy Pausch's Last Lecture.

This isn't really about firing customers.

The smarter move? Add a PITA premium; a "Pain In The Ass" surcharge.

For high-friction clients, raise the price until the margin justifies the hassle.

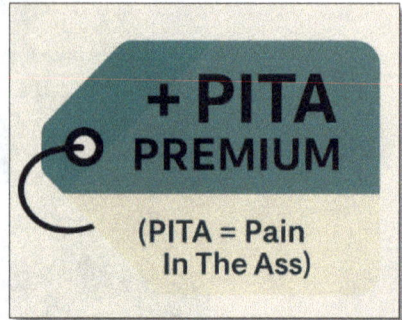

+PITA PREMIUM

(PITA = Pain In The Ass)

If they stay, they're finally worth it. If they leave, you just freed up your time and sanity.

Either way, you win.

Are you ready to start firing customers? Ever audited your customer base?

You might be surprised how much time you're spending on the wrong ones.

Do the math. Make the call.

Letting go isn't failure. It's focus. The best businesses aren't built by pleasing everyone. They're built by serving the right ones, well.

Original post URL: https://bradpoulos.com/firing-customers/

Why "No" Is the Second-Best Word a Salesperson Can Hear

Originally posted on June 23, 2025.

The Power of Clarity in Sales

I'll never forget the first time I heard the phrase, "What part of 'no' don't you understand?" It was the early '90s. I was a sales manager on a call with one of my reps, meeting the Director of IT and Telecom at a major Canadian retailer. I was pushing a bit too hard, and he cut me off with: "Brad, what part of no don't you understand?" At the time, it felt like a slap in the face. Now, I see it was the most respectful thing he could've said. In sales, "yes" is obviously the word you want to hear. But the second-best word? It's "no."

Why "Maybe" Is the Real Problem

"No" saves time. It brings clarity. It allows you to move on. "Maybe," on the other hand, traps you in limbo. When a prospect can't or won't make a decision, or simply avoids the discomfort of telling you the truth, you get stuck in a cycle of vague promises and never-ending follow-ups. Your calendar fills with non-productive check-ins, and your mental energy drains away as you wonder if the deal still has a pulse. Hearing "no" might sting, but it's also freeing. It provides closure. It helps you prioritize more promising leads and maintain a lean and accurate sales pipeline. The ability to spot dead ends quickly is one of the most valuable skills a salesperson can develop.

Why this matters: The Full Funnel Illusion

Many salespeople confuse a full pipeline with a healthy one. But if we're honest, most pipelines are bloated with deals that should've been disqualified long ago. Zig Ziglar once made this point using a closet analogy. You might look inside and see 14 suits. You're happy because it looks like you have plenty of options.

But take a closer look.

A few of those suits are worn, several are out of style, and at least one no longer fits. When the dust settles, you've really only got three wearable options, and one's a bit snug.

That's what most sales funnels look like. Full of "maybes." You'd be doing your psyche a favour by just getting rid of them.

WHAT YOU THINK YOUR FUNNEL LOOKS LIKE	WHAT IT ACTUALLY LOOKS LIKE
14 PROSPECTS. LOOKS GOOD ON PAPER.	3 REAL OPPORTUNITIES. ONE'S A BIT SNUG.

Saying "No" Is Hard—But Hearing It Is Underrated

Most of us already know that *saying* no can be hard. It feels like letting someone down. But saying it often brings relief and a sense of honesty.

What's less obvious is how powerful it is to *hear* a clear "no." In sales, you're going to hear it a lot. Accept it. Welcome it. It's how you stay sane.

A respectful, unambiguous "no" shows your time is being respected. Ironically, it can even build trust. When a buyer gives you a direct answer instead of ghosting, it shows integrity. And it allows you to redirect your energy toward prospects who are actually in play.

The other thing is that you have to lose sometime.

> *"If you never lose a deal, you're probably suck as a salesperson!"*
> *– Brad Poulos*

Think about it. If you close every deal, you're probably going after only the safest, warmest, cuddliest prospects. You're not testing things. Growth comes from experimenting, and losing deals is a natural byproduct of that.

You're probably ALSO pricing too low if you never lose. If no one ever pushes back, it's a signal that you're leaving money on the table.

Losing Teaches You What Winning Can't.

Every "no" is data. It sharpens your pitch, positioning, and product. If you're not losing sometimes, you're not learning fast enough. Iron sharpens iron.

Sales Is About Sorting, Not Convincing

Great salespeople aren't in the persuasion business. They're in the sorting business. The skill lies in quickly identifying who is truly interested and who isn't.

The best sellers create safe exits for prospects. They use clear, non-pushy language. They ask questions designed to reveal intent, such as:

- "Is this something you can realistically prioritize this quarter?"
- "If this isn't a fit, are you okay if I close the file?"
- "Is this a real need, or more of a nice-to-have for your team?"

These kinds of questions make it easier for people to be honest, and that honesty is a gift.

Bottom Line: No Is Feedback

"No" isn't failure. It's a signal that lets you refine your focus, sharpen your messaging, and reallocate your time to opportunities that are actually alive. So yes, chase that "yes." But don't be afraid to celebrate a quick, clean "no" along the way. Your calendar (and your sanity) will thank you.

The ability to SAY "no" can be rare as well. Learn about "Radical Candor" and how it can change your communication for the better.

Original post URL: https://bradpoulos.com/the-value-of-no/

The Columbo: A Veteran Sales Tactic You Can Use Anywhere

Originally posted on July 5, 2025.

The $10 Million Question I Almost Didn't Ask

We'd worked with a multinational retailer for years but had only ever landed a few crumbs of their telecom budget. The principal contact there, Ed, was a tough nut to crack. We had just bid on, but lost, a nice piece of business with this client. This would have been a significant deal for us, and our management wasn't thrilled that I lost the deal to our arch competitor, Scientific Atlanta.

An Interesting Aside:

Shortly after we learned that our competitor had won the RFP, I was at our headquarters for a meeting of the entire management team, which consisted of about 50 people. The President singled me out in front of the whole room and asked about the deal, specifically why we had lost. He was trying to come across as being fair-minded with the question, but we all knew he was actually pissed at us for losing this bid.

I will never forget my answer to him. It just rolled off my tongue, "Larry, the one thing I can never protect you from is an irrational competitor." I will also never forget the looks on the faces of my peers and the senior managers. They were impressed with my quick wit and gumption. My boss told me later it was an epic moment.

Word on the street was that the customer's negotiations with our competitor were not going well, and they hadn't yet signed a contract. I called Ed and said I'd like to take him to dinner and a hockey game (we had seats in the first row and Ed was a monster Leafs fan!). No agenda. Just a thank you for their business (since we had those crumbs, after all, I could say this with impunity).

I waited until 1/2 way through the third period – a good three + hours since we'd met for dinner – to ask, "So, how is everything working out with Scientific Atlanta?"

Ed hesitated before finally confiding that they were not very happy with their decision, and there might be a way to revisit the RFP we had lost.

This is a variation on the Columbo – a move that veteran salespeople (and cops) use all the time to get information. In this case, it helped me land a $10 million contract and hugely increased my visibility and reputation in the company.

The Columbo

If you've ever watched Columbo — the 1970s detective show starring Peter Falk as the lovably disheveled Lieutenant Columbo — you know the move. The lieutenant would spend 20 minutes chatting casually with a suspect, half-bumbling his way through what looked like a routine conversation. Then, as he turned to leave, he'd pause, cock his head, and say:

"Oh... just one more thing..."

And that would be the moment everything shifted. Because the "just one more thing" wasn't small talk but rather it was the real reason he was there. This little tactic works in sales too, and out of respect to its namesake, I call it the "Columbo".

Here's how it plays out. You schedule a meeting — maybe it's a follow-up, a quick demo, a check-in call. Everyone relaxes. The discussion is productive but light. As the conversation wraps up and you're saying your thank-yous and goodbyes, you casually throw in:

"Hey, one more thing. Who handles onboarding your new franchisees?"

Or:

"By the way, are you doing anything different for trade shows this year? I have a few ideas that might help with lead capture."

And boom. That's the real conversation. It's not bait-and-switch. It's just smart sequencing.

Why It Works

There's psychology behind this. When the meeting is "official," people are guarded. They have their mental shields up. All of their objections are at the front of mind, and they're ready to say no, or to deflect. But as the meeting winds down, those shields drop. You're in the clear. The vibe is friendly, the threat level is low. We're now talking about when the Leafs will finally crack the code and win the Cup. That's when the "one more thing" can sneak in and land with less resistance. It feels unscripted, informal, and oddly trustworthy. It's a kind of head fake, to borrow Randy Pausch's term. The stated agenda isn't the real agenda — but that's what makes the real agenda easier to pursue.

Oh, One More Thing...

Did you see what I did there? The Columbo Move works because it feels like an afterthought—even though it's anything but. It's not manipulation. It's timing. Sometimes your most important question isn't the first one. It's the one you ask with your hand on the doorknob.

Original post URL: https://bradpoulos.com/columbo/

Slippery When Greased: Making Business Flow Effortlessly

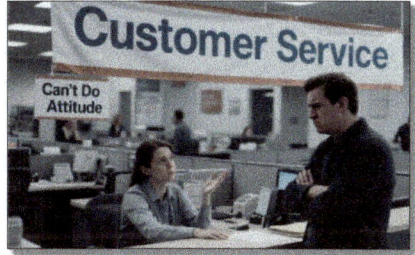

Originally posted on July 26, 2025.

It's no surprise, given where I spent a good deal of my career, that my go-to perspective is that of the salesperson. Even when in senior management, I spent a lot of time selling, if not to customers then to bankers, investors and partners. And while no one can benefit more from understanding this concept than someone in a sales role, it can be applied anywhere.

I call it the *Grease and Friction Framework*, and once you start seeing it, you'll find it's everywhere — in marketing, customer service, hiring, onboarding, operations, and even product design.

At its core, it's a simple concept:

- Grease is anything you do to make a desired outcome more likely.
- Friction is anything that gets in the way.

The salesperson has the most obvious opportunities to apply the framework. A good salesperson might offer a limited-time discount, a free trial, or a money-back guarantee as grease to move the buyer to a "yes". They anticipate objections and address them before they arise. They handle all the logistics so the customer barely has to lift a finger. That's grease.

On the flip side, friction shows up any time the customer hits a bump: a clunky checkout form, a confusing pitch, a delay in follow-up, crappy credit terms, or too many hoops to jump through. In a retail setting, friction might look like long lines, poor signage, a lack of helpful staff, or convoluted return policies.

My favourite pizza joint is a "mom and pop", independent shop that's been in business since 1967. Their pizza is amazingly tasty. Both the crust and the sauce are extraordinary, which is, after all, the foundation of a good pizza. Unfortunately, their business processes have also been around since 1967. Every time you call — yes, call. Web ordering? Fuggedaboudit! You have to give them your phone number, name and address. Every time! What? No call display? No POS system? Not even an Excel spreadsheet!

And then consider my part-time employer, Toronto Metropolitan University, which operates several cafes and cafeterias, none of which accept cash. I'm sure some overly progressive committee decided this was somehow "better" (using the incomprehensible criteria of a university), but there is one group that this is in no way "better" for — customers!

Removing Friction

Here's one small way I've used this concept outside of the sales environment. I offer downloadable tools on my website (things like Excel models, templates, and checklists), and I *want* people to download them and use them. If I make them available with no strings attached, then anyone can simply click and download. That's minimal friction, and what I've chosen to do for now.

If I ask for an email address first, that's a bit of friction, and at the margin, a few people won't bother. If I ask for name, phone number, business size, and what their favourite dinosaur is, I've created so much friction that most people won't bother. The more friction I introduce, the more people I lose. Every added step is a filter, whether I want it to be or not.

You can even apply this concept to yourself. Imagine you're trying to build a daily writing habit. If your workspace is cluttered, your writing tools are scattered, and you have to hunt for your notebook or charger every morning, that's friction. It makes it harder to get started and easier to procrastinate. But if you set up a dedicated spot with your laptop charged, your favourite pen and notebook ready, and a clear plan for what you'll write, you're adding grease. By removing obstacles and making it as easy as possible to start, you increase the likelihood that you'll stick with your habit and accomplish meaningful work.

Friction isn't Always Bad

Friction can sometimes serve a purpose. If I only want highly qualified leads, asking for more information may be worthwhile. If I want people who are really serious, adding friction might be a deliberate tactic. Friction can be strategic — as long as it's intentional.

Grease, too, isn't just about giving things away or making it "easy." That's a somewhat lazy way to sell (and less profitable). Grease can be about clarity.

Good copywriting is grease. A clean, fast-loading website is grease. A thoughtful onboarding sequence is grease. So is removing jargon, simplifying pricing, or showing a quick demo video.

Grease is also removing any impediments to closing in a B-to-B sales situation. You need to get a sign-off from your boss? No problem; let me have our VP give her a call and answer any questions she might have. You aren't sure of the business case? I have a white paper that you can share, detailing how five other firms have implemented our solution and saved significant headcount as a result. A savvy salesperson anticipates and works around these issues, helping the buyer navigate their own internal roadblocks so they can confidently say yes and allow the sale to close.

This framework also helps you diagnose problems. If people aren't taking the action you want — buying, signing up, sharing, referring — ask yourself:

- Where might the friction be?
- Could I add some grease?

In many cases, the answer is yes. Your payment flow might have too many steps. Your lead capture form might be asking for too much. Your website might be slow or confusing. You might not be following up fast enough.

Small businesses, in particular, can benefit from this mindset. You may not have a huge marketing budget or a big sales team, but you *can* make things smoother for your customers. You *can* identify and reduce friction. And you *can* grease the wheels so that more people do what you hope they'll do.

Grease and friction are everywhere — in how you hire, how you train, how you communicate. Think about your business processes through this lens and you'll start seeing opportunities you didn't notice before.

- What "rules" do you have in place that don't serve a purpose, or don't warrant the friction they introduce?
- What approval processes do we have, and are they appropriate?
- What information are we collecting and do we need it?
- Where are people falling out of our sales funnel?

Here's your takeaway:

> *Anything that slows, confuses, or annoys is friction. Anything that guides, encourages, or simplifies is grease.*

Use this lens. Ask the questions. And remember: every step you remove, every barrier you ease, and every helpful nudge you offer boosts your chances of getting the result you're aiming for.

Original post URL: https://bradpoulos.com/grease-vs-friction/

Referrals Are Great – But Not a Growth Strategy

Originally posted on August 2, 2025.

Why Relying on Word-of-Mouth Will Eventually Let You Down

You're doing great work, clients are happy, and then—bingo!—an email from a promising prospect pops into your inbox with the mellifluous subject line: "Andrea over at ABC Wholesale said I should call you."

Feels amazing, right? Until it doesn't.

Referrals are the gold standard of validation—high-trust, low-friction, and pre-warmed thanks to the inherent endorsement. It's tempting to build your whole business around them. But

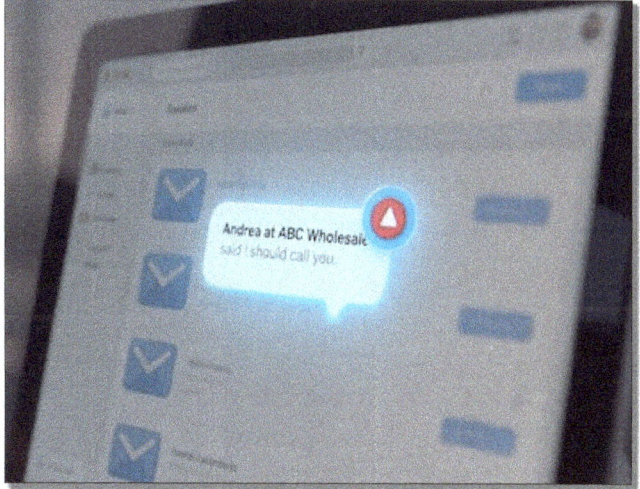

here's the problem: referrals are not a growth strategy.

They're a bonus, not a plan.

When you build your business on referrals alone, you give up control of your pipeline and you surrender your growth to the whims of others. That might work when you're busy and booked. But what happens when the phone stops ringing?

The Hidden Problems with Referral Dependence

1. You Can't Control Them
   Referrals show up when they show up. There's no way to schedule or forecast them. You can't run campaigns around them or scale them with consistency. That makes them unreliable as your primary source of leads.

2. You Take What You Get
   When you're living off referrals, you're often taking clients out of obligation rather than intention. Sometimes you'd rather not have the client. They don't fit, but you feel pressure to say yes. You don't want to seem ungrateful to the person who referred them.

3. You Don't Develop Core Marketing Muscles
   You can get lazy if you're not regularly having to articulate your value proposition, and test it. Things change. Messaging can get stale, and you're not maintaining assets like a landing page, lead magnet, or other marketing materials, and you're neglecting your own brand equity.

4. You'll Plateau
   A referral-only based business will hit a ceiling. Suddenly, the "nice to have" marketing work becomes urgent, and you're scrambling to catch up.

5. Tit for Tat
   Sometimes referrals come with strings attached. A partner sends you a lead, and there's a tacit expectation that you'll return the favour. This kind of quid pro quo is normal in most networking groups. Admittedly, most focus on micro-businesses and solopreneurs, but some take in larger operations.

And then there's the emotional cost. When you feel you owe someone a lead—or they think you do—it creates subtle tension. You start filtering decisions through a sense of debt or loyalty rather than what's actually best for your business. Over time, that corrodes your independence and clouds your judgment. What starts as friendly collaboration can quietly become a trap.

What to Do Instead (Without Abandoning Referrals)

Referrals aren't bad. They just shouldn't be the whole plan. Here's how to round out your strategy:

Build a Simple Marketing Engine

You don't need a full-blown funnel. Just pick one channel and make it work: write a monthly email, publish two useful blog posts, run a low-budget Google ad. As long as it's something you control.

Marketing doesn't have to be loud or pushy. Quiet consistency wins. When you show up regularly—even in small ways—

you start building visibility, credibility, and most importantly, momentum.

Ask for Referrals More Strategically

Referrals don't have to be passive. Ask for them after a great result. Make it easy—give clients an email they can forward or a landing page to share. Be specific about who you're looking for. The key is to frame it as a service, not a favour. "If you know someone else struggling with [problem], feel free to pass along my info. I'd love to help." That puts the emphasis on their network, not your need.

Turn Success into Proof

Every happy customer is an opportunity to create a testimonial, a case study, or even just a great quote. These stories build trust with people who don't know you yet. You're not just delivering results—you're building proof of reliability. The more you showcase that, the easier it becomes for strangers to say yes.

Create a Presence Beyond Your Network

Set up a basic website that speaks to your ideal customer. Start collecting emails. Post once a week on LinkedIn. You don't need to go viral; you just need to be discoverable. This doesn't mean turning into a content machine. It just means making sure that when someone does look you up, they see signs of life, credibility, and clarity. A digital footprint that says you're open for business.

Referrals Are a Bonus, Not a Business Plan

A steady stream of referrals is a great sign that you're doing something right. But it's not a foundation you can build on forever. If your next customer is always in someone else's hands, then so is your future. Build the kind of lasting business where referrals are the icing and not the cake. When they come in, it's a win... not a lifeline.

Original post URL: https://bradpoulos.com/referral-based-businesses/

The Lean Marketing Machine: 7 Hacks to Grow Your Small Business Fast

Originally posted on August 5, 2025.

Running a small business means you're constantly balancing ambition with reality. Your marketing budget is tight, but your creativity abounds. The truth is, you don't need a massive team or a six-figure ad spend to make a real impact. You need a willingness to try new things, experiment, and squeeze every drop of value from your efforts.

Here are seven marketing hacks designed for scrappy business owners who want results without waste. Whether you're just starting out or looking to get more from your current marketing, pick one or two of these ideas and put them to work this week.

1. Turn One Idea Into Ten Pieces of Content

Think about the last blog post you wrote. Did you squeeze all the value out of it? Most small businesses create a piece of content, post it once, and move on. But that single idea can be repurposed in a dozen different ways. Turn that blog post into a short Instagram Reel, a LinkedIn carousel, a tweet thread, a quote graphic, an email to your list, a YouTube Short, a podcast snippet, a TikTok (if you're feeling adventurous), a Reddit post, and an SEO-optimized article for your website.

The key is to create once and distribute everywhere. Your audience isn't all hanging out in the same place, so your content shouldn't be either. Tools like Repurpose.io (pricey) or ContentFries (affordable) can help you automate and streamline this process, making it easier than ever to get your message out across multiple platforms

2. Make Friends with the Algorithm

You don't need to be an influencer to win on social media, but you do need to play by the platform's rules. Right now, short-form videos like Reels and Shorts get the most organic reach. Carousels still work on LinkedIn and Instagram, and interactive posts—think polls, questions, and behind-the-scenes moments—spark real engagement.

Algorithms love consistency. Start simple: one useful, unscripted video a week. It doesn't have to be polished; just be real. The more you show up, the faster your audience gets to know, like, and trust you. And on social media, consistency beats perfection every time.

3. Ask Your Customers to Create the Content

User-generated content (UGC) is marketing gold, and your customers are sitting on a treasure chest. People trust what other buyers say way more than anything from the company, so invite them to share the love: unboxing videos, before-and-after pics, or a quick story about how they use your stuff. Sweeten the deal with a small reward, or just give them a shoutout in your newsletter or on socials. Make it fun and easy with a hashtag like #MyEastviewBuild, and watch your community do the marketing for you. Remember: your customers are your coolest brand ambassadors. Hand them the mic.

4. Slide into the DMs (Tactfully)

Social platforms are built for connection, so use them to actually connect. Make it a habit to start five to ten meaningful conversations every day. Thank someone for commenting on your post, reply to a Story with a genuine compliment, or follow up with someone who liked or reshared your content. The key here is to build relationships, not pitch your product. When you focus on being social first, you'll be top of mind when your connections are ready to buy. Social selling works best when you act like a real person, not a sales robot.

5. Trade Your Skills, Not Your Cash

If your budget is tight, get creative with bartering. Offer your services in exchange for something you need. Maybe you're a bookkeeper who can help a graphic designer in exchange for a new website. Or a landscaper who trades services for business cards. Or a café that supplies lunch to a videographer in exchange for promo clips. Bartering is old-school, but it still works. When cash flow is tight, trading skills can help you get what you need without spending a dime.

6. Dare to be Different, and Show It!

Vanilla doesn't stand out. What's quirky, bold, or unexpected about you or your business? That's the stuff worth sharing. Maybe it's your origin story told as a comic strip, the "we almost gave up" moment captured in a Reel, or the outtakes from your last photoshoot. Don't be afraid to share your imperfections. One florist went viral by posting "bouquet fails" with the hashtag #FloralFlops, and ended up doubling their orders. Your quirks and mistakes are often your superpower. Embrace them.

7. Become a PR Machine (Without Hiring One)

You don't need a fancy PR agency to get media coverage. Local media, niche podcasts, and newsletters are always looking for interesting stories. Pitch them with headlines like, "How we bounced back after losing our biggest customer," "Why our tiny team beat out three big competitors," or "We grew 300% with zero ad spend—here's how." Write your pitch like a headline and include the full story in your email. Keep it short, visual, and human.

Smart, Human Marketing on a Shoestring

Marketing doesn't have to be expensive, but it does have to be intentional. Be human. Be helpful. Be consistent. If you try even one of these hacks this week, you're already ahead of most small business owners.

Original post URL: https://bradpoulos.com/marketing-hacks/

Jobs to Be Done: Understanding What Your Customers Really Want

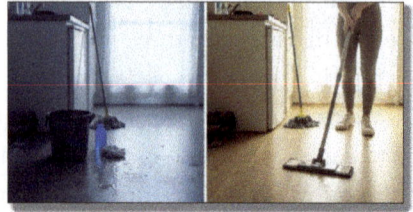

Originally posted on October 21, 2025.

People don't want a drill. They want a hole in the wall. Most businesses don't really understand why their customers buy from them. They think they know. They've got demographics. They've analyzed seasonal purchase patterns. They've even done customer surveys where people check boxes about "quality" and "value." But they're looking at the wrong data entirely. Because here's the thing. If you're in the drill business, obsessing over chuck sizes and battery life, you're not playing big-league marketing. Look more deeply into what customers are really buying.

The Theory That Explains Why Good Companies Fail

Successful companies are consistently, even when they're doing everything "right." They listen to customers, invest in R&D, and improve their products. And yet they still get blindsided. The problem? They're measuring success by the wrong yardstick.

Companies segment customers by demographics and product attributes: "35-year-old males who want faster processing speeds." But these categories don't predict actual buying behaviour.

Clayton Christensen, author of *The Innovator's Dilemma* and *Competing Against Luck*, focused his research on innovation and disruption. Along with Bob Moesta and colleagues at The Re-Wired Group, he worked with a client in the fast food industry that wanted to sell more milkshakes. They'd done the traditional market research: improved the product based on customer feedback, tweaked the formula, played with pricing. Sales stayed flat.

So Christensen's team tried something different. They stood in restaurants for 18 hours asking people: "What job were you hiring that milkshake to do?"

Christensen realized that customers don't buy products, they "hire" them to make progress in specific circumstances.

This insight became "Jobs to Be Done" theory, and it emerged from one of the best consulting stories in business literature.

What this teaches us

Segmenting by occupation, age, gender, and other demographic variables won't reveal the motivations behind purchase behaviour. Behavioural variables, like the circumstances of use and the job to be done, run deeper and provide better positioning guidance. Two people may. be buying the same thing for very different reasons. Don't miss the nuance.

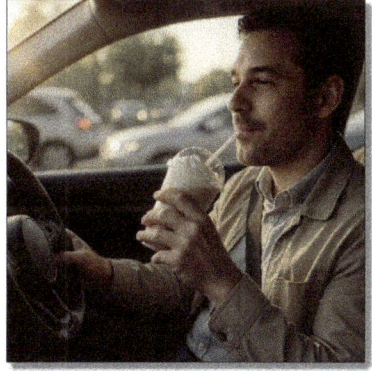

Identifying the true competition will include indirect competitors you might not have considered, as well as customer workarounds. Even non-consumption should be considered a form of competition—because the customer might simply choose to do nothing.

Take tax software, for example. Before products like TurboTax, many people either paid expensive accountants for simple returns or muddled through paper forms, confused and anxious. Others just didn't file properly at all. TurboTax didn't just compete with accountants: it activated non-consumers by lowering the barrier to entry and making the process approachable.

Why This Matters for Your Business

Successful companies march upmarket, adding features and improving performance along dimensions that matter to existing customers. It's what business school teaches. It's also what makes them vulnerable.

Jobs to Be Done keeps you from falling into this trap in three ways:

First, it reveals non-consumption. Your biggest opportunity might not be stealing customers from competitors—it's serving people who've cobbled together inadequate workarounds. They're doing the job badly or not at all because nothing serves them well.

Second, it prevents feature creep. You stop gold-plating your product with bells and whistles nobody wanted. That premium coffee grinder with seventeen settings? If the job is "make decent coffee before I'm fully awake," those extra features are just friction.

Think about how remote controls went from simple channel changers to overly complex gadgets with dozens of rarely used buttons.

Third, it predicts actual switching behaviour. Traditional market research asks, "Would you buy this?" JTBD asks, "What progress are you trying to make, and what are you currently using?"

The gap between those answers is where opportunity lives.

You'll also uncover opportunities for invention and innovation. Those people using inadequate Band-Aids are ripe targets for game changers. Think about how the Swiffer redefined the category from "mop" to "quick, lightweight cleaning in small bursts without setup", and how Uber changed the game from taxis to safe, reliable, transparent, on-demand personal mobility.

How to Find Your Customers' Jobs (And Go Deeper Than You Think)

Stop asking what features they want. Start asking about the last time they used your product or service and what they were trying to accomplish. What else did they consider using? What would have happened if they couldn't do this? How did they feel before, during, and after?

Pay attention to three dimensions: functional (what tangible outcome do they need?), emotional (how do they want to feel?), and social (how does this affect how others see them?).

But here's the advanced move: don't stop at the first answer. Use what marketers call "laddering" and what my colleagues and I just call the "5 whys". Keep asking "why does that matter to you?" to climb from surface-level features to deeper truths.

A customer says they hired your accounting service to "file taxes correctly" (functional job). Fine. Now, ladder up:

Why does filing taxes matter? → "To avoid IRS problems."

Why do IRS problems matter? → "There are financial and personal repercussions"

Why does that matter? → "Because I'm terrified of jail and losing everything

I've built."

See what happened? You started with tax compliance and discovered the real job is peace of mind and protection of their life's work. If you think about it, how could anyone really need to file their taxes. It's more like we have to! That distinction change everything about how you market and deliver your service. You're not selling tax prep. You're selling freedom from anxiety.

The Mistakes Everyone Makes

Don't confuse demographics with jobs. "Millennials" aren't consuming your product just because they share a birth year. A 28-year-old buying a milkshake for their morning commute has more in common with a 52-year-old doing the same job than with another 28-year-old getting it to shut up their kid.

And don't assume the job never changes. The pandemic radically shifted what people looked to restaurants to do. Suddenly the job became "help me feel normal" or "give me a break from cooking," not "provide a place to gather."

Forces of Progress

Going a bit deeper into the theory reveals the emotional and psychological dynamics that influence customers when deciding whether to adopt or abandon a product or service.

There is an interplay of motivations that explains why people switch to your product (or why they don't, even when yours is objectively better). Bob Moesta and Chris Spiek (building on Christensen's work) identified four forces at play in every purchase decision involving potential change.

The push of the current situation's inadequacies, and the pull of the new product's promise, are forces for change that move the customer toward the new choice. The fears and uncertainty about switching and comfort with the current way of doing things, even if it's imperfect ("devil you know"), are the forces against change, leading the customer to stay put.

Change or progress happens when: Push + Pull > Anxiety + Habit

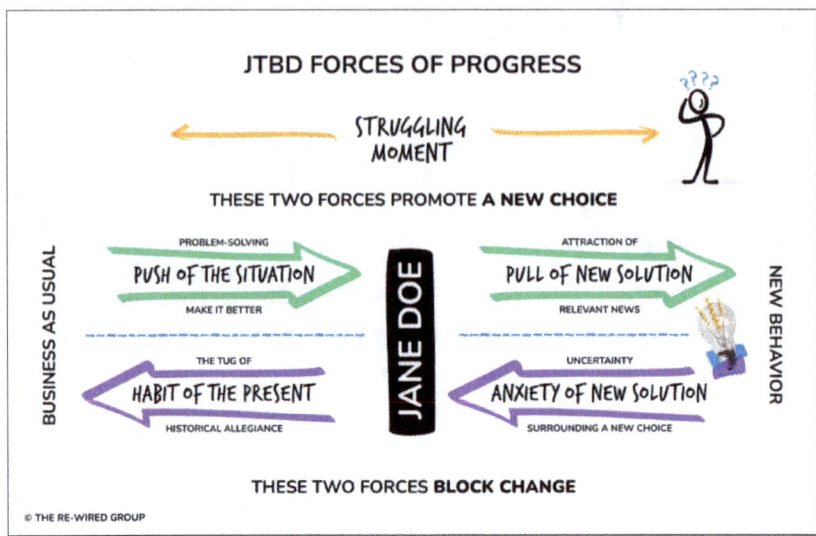

How to Put This to Work

Most marketers only focus on Pull (making their product attractive). But that's just 1 of 4 forces. If you ignore the others, you'll wonder why your "obviously superior" product isn't selling.

Interview customers who to gain insight about each of the four forces. Don't just ask why they bought yours or another solution. Go deeper. Use the "five why's" and search for motivation stemming from each of the four forces.

Your promotional activity and positioning should be tailored based on the evidence you gather. Which forces are most favourable to you? Your promotional activity should amplify those. And don't be afraid to agitate the problem. Show the cost of staying put, not just in money but time, stress, and missed opportunities.

You also need to design your offering around the forces that determine whether someone actually switches. Free trials reduce anxiety. Quick wins amplify pull before doubt creeps in. Comparison charts amplify push by making the status quo feel expensive.

The trickiest force is habit. People stick with terrible solutions because switching feels exhausting. This is why migration support matters. Import tools and data transfer don't just reduce anxiety; they demolish the practical barriers that make habit so powerful. Smart businesses engineer their entire customer journey around these forces, not just their product features.

The Big Mistake

Most failed products have strong pull (great features) but ignore anxiety and habit. The iPhone succeeded partly because it reduced anxiety (intuitive enough that you didn't need a manual) and habit (kept familiar concepts like "home button" and "apps").

WeWork struggled because even though push was strong (people hate traditional offices) and pull was strong (cool spaces), anxiety was massive (long-term commitment, what if we outgrow it?) and habit was huge (commercial real estate is how things are done).

Your Assignment

This week, interview one customer. Not a survey. But an actual conversation. Ask about the last time they bought from you. Ask what they almost bought instead. Ask what would have happened if your business didn't exist.

Then ladder up. Keep asking "why does that matter?" until you hit something that makes them pause. That's usually where the real job lives.

You'll learn more in that 20-minute conversation than from a thousand surveys about how they'd rate your "customer service" on a scale of 1 to 10.

Because once you understand the job you're really being hired to do, everything else—your marketing, your product development, your pricing— suddenly gets a lot clearer.

Original post URL: https://bradpoulos.com/jobs-to-be-done/

About the Author

Brad Poulos is an entrepreneur, educator, and advisor based near Toronto, Canada, with experience leading and supporting businesses in the telecom, software, and cannabis industries. Over the past 40 years, he's worked in corporate roles, scaled a startup to #8 on the Profit 100 list, taken a company public, and helped launch and grow multiple ventures as a founder, investor, and advisor.

Brad holds an Electronics Technologist Diploma from DeVry and an MBA from the Ivey Business School. Today, he teaches entrepreneurship, small business management, and strategy at Toronto Metropolitan University, where he also created Canada's first university-level cannabis business course. His work focuses on helping founders and owners create and execute strategy that leads to focused, profitable companies.

Outside the classroom, Brad writes and appears in the media about small business, plays keyboards in Southpawz, a classic rock band, trains in Taekwondo, and golfs whenever possible. He's a proud father, uncle, and grandfather, happiest when sharing a good story or a new adventure.

Index

www.ingramcontent.com/pod-product-compliance
Lightning Source LLC
Chambersburg PA
CBHW061158240326
R18026600001B/R180266PG41519CBX00032B/7